Grade **2**

Pearson Scott Foresman

Leveled Reader
Teaching Guide

W9-CFH-027

PEARSON

Glenview, Illinois • Boston, Massachusetts • Chandler, Arizona • Upper Saddle River, New Jersey

ISBN: 13: 978-0-328-48441-6
ISBN: 10:   0-328-48441-5
9 10 V039 15 14
CC1

Table of Contents

LEVELED READER TITLE	Instruction	Comprehension Practice	Vocabulary Practice
The New Kid in Bali	12–13	14	15
An Astronaut Space Walk	16–17	18	19
Camping at Crescent Lake	20–21	22	23
Desert Animals	24–25	26	27
Glooskap and the First Summer: An Algonquin Tale	28–29	30	31
Be Ready for an Emergency	32–33	34	35
Let's Work Together!	36–37	38	39
Farming Families	40–41	42	43
Growing Up	44–45	46	47
Showing Good Manners	48–49	50	51
Dotty's Art	52–53	54	55
Living in Seoul	56–57	58	59
Arachnid or Insect?	60–61	62	63
The International Food Fair!	64–65	66	67
Thomas Adams: Chewing Gum Inventor	68–69	70	71
Making Travel Fun	72–73	74	75

Graphic Organizers

Introduction

Scott Foresman *Reading Street* provides more than 750 leveled readers that help children become better readers and build a lifelong love of reading. The *Reading Street* leveled readers are engaging texts that help children practice critical reading skills and strategies. They also provide opportunities to build vocabulary, understand concepts, and develop reading fluency.

The leveled readers were developed to be age-appropriate and appealing to children at each grade level. The leveled readers consist of engaging texts in a variety of genres, including fantasy, folk tales, realistic fiction, historical fiction, and narrative and expository nonfiction. To better address real-life reading skills that children will encounter in testing situations and beyond, a higher percentage of nonfiction texts is provided at each grade.

USING THE LEVELED READERS

You can use the leveled readers to meet the diverse needs of your children. Consider using the readers to

- practice critical skills and strategies
- build fluency
- build vocabulary and concepts
- build background for the main selections in the student book
- provide a variety of reading experiences, e.g., shared, group, individual, take-home, readers' theater

GUIDED READING APPROACH

The *Reading Street* leveled readers are leveled according to Guided Reading criteria by experts trained in Guided Reading. The Guided Reading levels increase in difficulty within a grade level and across grade levels. In addition to leveling according to Guided Reading criteria, the instruction provided in the *Leveled Reader Teaching Guide* is compatible with Guided Reading instruction. An instructional routine is provided for each leveled reader. This routine is most effective when working with individual children or small groups.

MANAGING THE CLASSROOM

When using the leveled readers with individuals or small groups, you'll want to keep the other children engaged in meaningful, independent learning tasks. Establishing independent practice stations throughout the classroom and child routines for these stations can help you manage the rest of the class while you work with individuals or small groups. Practice stations can include listening, phonics, vocabulary, independent reading, and cross-curricular activities. For classroom management, create a work board that lists the stations and which children should be at each station. Provide instructions at each station that detail the tasks to be accomplished. Update the board and alert children when they should rotate to a new station. For additional support for managing your classroom, see the *Reading Street* Practice Stations' *Classroom Management Handbook*.

USING THE LEVELED READER TEACHING GUIDE

The *Leveled Reader Teaching Guide* provides an instruction plan for each leveled reader based on the same instructional routine.

INTRODUCE THE BOOK The Introduction includes suggestions for creating interest in the text by discussing the title and author, building background, and previewing the book and its features.

READ THE BOOK Before children begin reading the book, have them set purposes for reading and discuss how they can use the reading strategy as they read. Determine how you want children in a particular group to read the text, softly or silently, to a specific point or the entire text. Then use the Comprehension Questions to provide support as needed and to assess comprehension.

REVISIT THE BOOK The Think and Share and Reader Response questions provide opportunities for children to demonstrate their understanding of the text, the target comprehension skill, and vocabulary. The Response Options require children to revisit the text to respond to what they've read and to move beyond the text to explore related content.

SKILL WORK The Skill Work box provides instruction and practice for the target skill and strategy and selection vocabulary. Instruction for an alternate comprehension skill allows teachers to provide additional skill instruction and practice for children.

USING THE GRAPHIC ORGANIZERS

Graphic organizers in blackline-master format can be found on pages 132–152. These can be used as overhead transparencies or as worksheets.

ASSESSING PERFORMANCE

Use the assessment forms that begin on page 6 to make notes about your children's reading skills, use of reading strategies, and general reading behaviors.

MEASURE FLUENT READING (pp. 6–7) Provides directions for measuring a child's fluency, based on words correct per minute (wcpm), and reading accuracy using a running record.

OBSERVATION CHECKLIST (p. 8) Allows you to note the regularity with which children demonstrate their understanding and use of reading skills and strategies.

READING BEHAVIORS CHECKLIST (p. 9) Provides criteria for monitoring certain reading behaviors.

READING STRATEGY ASSESSMENT (p. 10) Provides criteria for evaluating each child's proficiency as a strategic reader.

PROGRESS REPORT (p. 11) Provides a means to track a child's book-reading progress over a period of time by noting the level at which a child reads and his or her accuracy at that level. Reading the chart from left to right gives you a visual model of how quickly a child is making the transition from one level to the next. Share these reports with parents or guardians to help them see how their child's reading is progressing.

Measure
Fluent Reading

Taking a Running Record

A running record is an assessment of a child's oral reading accuracy and oral reading fluency. Reading accuracy is based on the number of words read correctly. Reading fluency is based on the reading rate (the number of words correct per minute) and the degree to which a child reads with a "natural flow."

How to Measure Reading Accuracy

1. Choose a grade-level text of about 80 to 120 words that is unfamiliar to the child.
2. Make a copy of the text for yourself. Make a copy for the child or have the child read aloud from a book.
3. Give the child the text and have the child read aloud. (You may wish to record the child's reading for later evaluation.)
4. On your copy of the text, mark any miscues or errors the child makes while reading. See the running record sample on page 7, which shows how to identify and mark miscues.
5. Count the total number of words in the text and the total number of errors made by the child. Note: If a child makes the same error more than once, such as mispronouncing the same word multiple times, count it as one error. Self-corrections do not count as actual errors. Use the following formula to calculate the percentage score, or accuracy rate:

$$\frac{\text{Total Number of Words} - \text{Total Number of Errors}}{\text{Total Number of Words}} \times 100 = \text{percentage score}$$

Interpreting the Results

- A child who reads **95–100%** of the words correctly is reading at an **independent level** and may need more challenging text.
- A child who reads **90–94%** of the words correctly is reading at an **instructional level** and will likely benefit from guided instruction.
- A child who reads **89%** or fewer of the words correctly is reading at a **frustrational level** and may benefit most from targeted instruction with lower-level texts and intervention.

How to Measure Reading Rate (WCPM)

1. Follow Steps 1–3 above.
2. Note the exact times when the child begins and finishes reading.
3. Use the following formula to calculate the number of words correct per minute (WCPM):

$$\frac{\text{Total Number of Words Read Correctly}}{\text{Total Number of Seconds}} \times 60 = \text{words correct per minute}$$

Interpreting the Results

By the end of the year, a second-grader should be reading approximately 90–100 WCPM.

Running Record Sample

Running Record Sample

Notations

Just then a fly crawled near Fred. **7**

Fred's long, sticky tongue shot out in a **15**

flash and caught the tiny insect. **21**

"Delicious! I'm full now," he said **27**

loudly. He had already eaten three other **34**

insects and a worm in the past hour. **42**

Frankie overheard Fred and climbed **47**

down a few branches. He moved **53**

quickly and easily without falling. **58**

"What are you doing, Fred?" he **64**

asked in a friendly voice. **69**

"I was just finishing up my lunch," **76**

Fred answered. "How is life up high **83**

today, my friend?" **86**

Accurate Reading
The child reads a word correctly.

Insertion
The child inserts words or parts of words that are not in the text.

Mispronunciation/Misreading
The child pronounces or reads a word incorrectly.

Hesitation
The child hesitates over a word, and the teacher provides the word. Wait several seconds before telling the child what the word is.

Self-correction
The child reads a word incorrectly but then corrects the error. Do not count self-corrections as actual errors. However, noting self-corrections will help you identify words the child finds difficult.

Omission
The child omits words or word parts.

Substitution
The child substitutes words or parts of words for the words in the text.

Running Record Results
Total Number of Words: **86**
Number of Errors: **5**

Reading Time: **64 seconds**

▶ **Reading Accuracy**

$\frac{86 - 5}{86}$ x 100 = 94.186 = 94%

Accuracy Percentage Score: **94%**

▶ **Reading Rate—WCPM**

$\frac{81}{64}$ x 60 = 75.9 = 76 words correct per minute

Reading Rate: **76 WCPM**

Observation Checklist

Child's Name _____ Date _____

Behaviors Observed	Always (Proficient)	Usually (Fluent)	Sometimes (Developing)	Rarely (Novice)
Reading Strategies and Skills				
Uses prior knowledge and preview to understand what book is about				
Makes predictions and checks them while reading				
Uses context clues to figure out meanings of new words				
Uses phonics and syllabication to decode words				
Self-corrects while reading				
Reads at an appropriate reading rate				
Reads with appropriate intonation and stress				
Uses fix-up strategies				
Identifies story elements: character, setting, plot, theme				
Summarizes plot or main ideas accurately				
Uses target comprehension skill to understand the text better				
Responds thoughtfully about the text				

Reading Behaviors and Attitudes				
Enjoys listening to stories				
Chooses reading as a free-time activity				
Reads with sustained interest and attention				
Participates in discussion about books				

General Comments

Reading Behaviors Checklist

Child's Name _____   Date _____

Behavior	Yes	No	Not Applicable
Recognizes letters of the alphabet			
Recognizes name in print			
Recognizes some environmental print, such as signs and logos			
Knows the difference between letters and words			
Knows the difference between capital and lowercase letters			
Understands function of capitalization and punctuation			
Recognizes that book parts, such as the cover, title page, and table of contents, offer information			
Recognizes that words are represented in writing by specific sequences of letters			
Recognizes words that rhyme			
Distinguishes rhyming and nonrhyming words			
Knows letter-sound correspondences			
Identifies and isolates initial sounds in words			
Identifies and isolates final sounds in words			
Blends sounds to make spoken words			
Segments one-syllable spoken words into individual phonemes			
Reads consonant blends and digraphs			
Reads and understands endings, such as *-es, -ed, -ing*			
Reads vowels and vowel diphthongs			
Reads and understands possessives			
Reads and understands compound words			
Reads simple sentences			
Reads simple stories			
Understands simple story structure			
Other:			

Reading Strategy Assessment

Child _____ Date _____

Teacher _____

		Proficient	Developing	Emerging	Not showing trait
Building Background Comments:	Previews	☐	☐	☐	☐
	Asks questions	☐	☐	☐	☐
	Predicts	☐	☐	☐	☐
	Activates prior knowledge	☐	☐	☐	☐
	Sets own purposes for reading	☐	☐	☐	☐
	Other:	☐	☐	☐	☐
Comprehension Comments:	Retells/summarizes	☐	☐	☐	☐
	Questions, evaluates ideas	☐	☐	☐	☐
	Relates to self/other texts	☐	☐	☐	☐
	Paraphrases	☐	☐	☐	☐
	Rereads/reads ahead for meaning	☐	☐	☐	☐
	Visualizes	☐	☐	☐	☐
	Uses decoding strategies	☐	☐	☐	☐
	Uses vocabulary strategies	☐	☐	☐	☐
	Understands key ideas of a text	☐	☐	☐	☐
	Other:	☐	☐	☐	☐
Fluency Comments:	Adjusts reading rate	☐	☐	☐	☐
	Reads for accuracy	☐	☐	☐	☐
	Uses expression	☐	☐	☐	☐
	Other:	☐	☐	☐	☐
Connections Comments:	Relates text to self	☐	☐	☐	☐
	Relates text to text	☐	☐	☐	☐
	Relates text to world	☐	☐	☐	☐
	Other:	☐	☐	☐	☐
Self-Assessment Comments:	Is aware of: Strengths	☐	☐	☐	☐
	Needs	☐	☐	☐	☐
	Improvement/achievement	☐	☐	☐	☐
	Sets and implements learning goals	☐	☐	☐	☐
	Maintains logs, records, portfolio	☐	☐	☐	☐
	Works with others	☐	☐	☐	☐
	Shares ideas and materials	☐	☐	☐	☐
	Other:	☐	☐	☐	☐

Progress Report

Child's Name _____

At the top of the chart, record the book title, its grade/unit/week (for example, 1.2.3), and the child's accuracy percentage. See page 6 for measuring fluency, calculating accuracy and reading rates. At the bottom of the chart, record the date you took the running record. In the middle of the chart, make an X in the box across from the level of the child's reading—frustrational level (below 89% accuracy), instructional level (90–94% accuracy), or independent level (95–100% accuracy). Record the reading rate (WCPM) in the next row.

Book Title						
Grade/Unit/Week						
Reading Accuracy Percentage						
LEVEL	**Frustrational** (89% or below)					
	Instructional (90–94%)					
	Independent (95% or above)					
Reading Rate (WCPM)						
Date						

The New Kid in Bali

SUMMARY Children read about Denny's summer in Indonesia. He learns that being different can mean being special. Children explore character as they read clues about Denny's character traits. They also see that a story can have two settings.

LESSON VOCABULARY

beautiful	country
friend	front
someone	somewhere

INTRODUCE THE BOOK

INTRODUCE THE TITLE AND AUTHOR Discuss the title and the author of *The New Kid in Bali*. Ask children to look at the illustration on the cover and comment on how it relates to the title. Ask children how the story may relate to social studies.

BUILD BACKGROUND Elicit a discussion about moving and traveling to a new place. Ask: Where did you travel or move to? How did you feel before you left? How did you feel when you were there? If you returned, how did you feel when you returned? Do you want to go back?

PREVIEW/USE ILLUSTRATIONS As children look through the book at the illustrations, encourage them to think about the genre, characters, and setting. Ask: Do you think this story could happen? Who is the new kid? Do the pictures give you clues about where the story takes place? Do the events in the story happen in one place?

READ THE BOOK

SET PURPOSE Model how to *set a purpose* for reading. Say: "From the illustration on the cover, it looks like the children are somewhere warm. The buildings look unusual. Maybe they are somewhere far away. I want to read on and find out more about where the story takes place."

STRATEGY SUPPORT: MONITOR AND CLARIFY Explain to children that good readers know that what they read must make sense. Explain that they should check as they read to make sure they understand what they are reading. Model questions to ask while reading: What does this mean? Does this make sense? Do I understand this?

COMPREHENSION QUESTIONS

PAGE 3 How do you think Denny made new friends? *(by playing soccer)*

PAGE 4 How do you think Denny helped his parents? *(He ordered food for them.)*

PAGE 5 Who picked up Bali customs faster, Denny or his parents? *(Denny)*

PAGE 7 Describe what a living room in a *rumah* was like. *(Possible response: It would have a roof and some furniture, but no walls.)*

PAGE 9 How are a temple and a church similar? *(Possible responses: Families go there; they have events; it is a place for people to meet.)*

PAGE 10 What did you learn about Denny on this page? *(Possible responses: He lives in California; he is in second grade.)*

REVISIT THE BOOK

THINK AND SHARE

1. Bali and California
2. Possible responses given.
   Bali: speak Indonesian, eat with fingers, each room is a building, temples; California: speak English, eat with a fork, house has many rooms in one building, churches; Both: play soccer, have fun with friends and family
3. Possible responses should include all the words with short vowels on the page. Children who choose the same page can compare their lists.
4. Possible responses: Everything could be different. The language, the food, the houses, and the neighborhoods could all be different.

EXTEND UNDERSTANDING Describe *theme* as the big idea of the story. Discuss the theme by asking children how Denny's feelings about being the new kid changed during the story. Prompt children to relate their personal experiences of being afraid of something new or liking something new to the text. Lead them to see the theme—being new or different can be a positive experience.

RESPONSE OPTIONS

WRITING Have children write a short paragraph about their experiences trying something very new and different.

SOCIAL STUDIES CONNECTION

Time For SOCIAL STUDIES

The puppet show that Denny saw at the temple in Bali may have used shadow puppets. Arrange with your librarian to have books with pictures of this intricate art form. Shadow puppet shows are generally about Indonesian myths. You may wish to read one of these myths to your class.

Skill Work

TEACH/REVIEW VOCABULARY

Play vocabulary memory. Write each word and its definition on separate index cards. Place them writing-side-down in rows. Have children take turns turning over two cards at a time. Children earn points by matching a word to its definition.

ELL Play vocabulary charades. Pair English language learners with proficient English speakers. Assign each pair of children a different vocabulary word. Give children time to decide how to act out the words.

TARGET SKILL AND STRATEGY

CHARACTER AND SETTING Explain to children that authors tell them what the *characters* are like in the story. After children read page 3, pause and ask volunteers to describe character traits of the main character. Ask: What is the main character's name? What sport does he play? As children read, invite them to respond when they notice new character traits about Denny. After reading, have children describe the *setting*. Explain that the setting is both the time and place of the story. Setting can be real or imaginary. Ask children to recall the two places in the story. Then ask children when the story took place. Ask: Did the story happen a long time ago, or could it happen today?

MONITOR AND CLARIFY Remind children to stop and clarify if they don't understand what they are reading. Model questions to ask: What does this mean? Do I understand this? Explain to children that a dictionary might help them figure out unknown words. Remind children that checking their understanding and using a dictionary will help them as they read.

ADDITIONAL SKILL INSTRUCTION

PLOT Have children think about *plot* by asking them what events happened in the story. Write their responses on separate pieces of paper. Then have them put the events in order of what happened at the beginning, the middle, and the end of the story.

Name _____

Character and Setting

Read the paragraphs.

Look for words that tell you about the setting. Write these words under Setting.

Then, look for words that tell you about the character, Denny. Write these words under Character.

> When Dad got the job I was glad. I like traveling with my family to see new places. I like the adventure of going to different places, even if I have to be the new kid there.
>
> Dad helps out on small farms around the world. This summer we went to the island country of Bali. Kids speak Indonesian there. They eat meals with their fingers. And best of all, they love soccer, just like at home!

Setting

_____
_____
_____
_____
_____
_____
_____
_____
_____

Character

_____
_____
_____
_____
_____
_____
_____
_____
_____

Vocabulary

Synonyms are words that have the same meaning. Draw lines to match the synonyms.

1. beautiful

2. country

3. friend

a. playmate—a child that plays with other children

b. pretty—pleasing to look at

c. nation—a large group of people that share the same government

4. Write a sentence with the word *someone*.

_____

- -

_____

- -

_____

5. Write a sentence with the word *somewhere*.

_____

- -

_____

- -

_____

An Astronaut Space Walk

SUMMARY This nonfiction book explains how astronauts in spacesuits use space walks to solve problems in space. It extends the lesson concept of why someone would want to explore space.

LESSON VOCABULARY

everywhere live
machines move
woman work
world

INTRODUCE THE BOOK

INTRODUCE THE TITLE AND AUTHOR Discuss with children the title and author of *An Astronaut Space Walk*. Explain that science includes learning about outer space. Ask: How does this book relate to science?

BUILD BACKGROUND Have children discuss what they know about survival in space. Ask: Do you need special ships or clothing to live in space? Why or why not?

PREVIEW/TAKE A PICTURE WALK Have children look at the photos and read the captions and labels in the book before reading. Explain that the captions tell what the photos are all about.

ELL Use the photos and captions to help children understand certain terms that are used in the book, such as *astronaut, pack, rockets, space, space station,* and *space walk*.

READ THE BOOK

SET PURPOSE Have children set a purpose for reading *An Astronaut Space Walk*. Remind children of what they discussed in the preview. Ask: Why would you like to read this book?

STRATEGY SUPPORT: TEXT STRUCTURE Tell the children that as they read, they will encounter descriptions of what astronauts do and how their spacesuit works to protect them. Have them note how the picture captions help clarify the text.

COMPREHENSION QUESTIONS

PAGE 3 Look at the photo. What do you think it feels like to wear a spacesuit? *(Possible response: It is hot, and it is hard to move your arms and legs.)*

PAGE 6 What is the main idea? *(A spacesuit solves many problems for astronauts in space.)*

PAGE 8 Why do astronauts use a special pack in space? *(It has rockets that help them move around in space.)*

PAGE 11 Astronauts sometimes bring objects from space back to Earth. What is a reason that astronauts might bring objects back to a spaceship? *(Possible response: to study them or to repair them)*

REVISIT THE BOOK

THINK AND SHARE

1. Possible response: Scientists and astronauts have made space walks an important part of exploring space.
2. Possible response: Page 4 shows an astronaut practicing what she will do on a space walk. Page 5 shows her on the space walk. Reading the captions helped me figure this out.
3. Possible responses: There is no air in *space. Astronauts* wear *spacesuits.*
4. Possible responses given. Problems: may be hot in space, hard to move in space, tools can float away. Solutions: water-cooled spacesuits, rocket packs, tools with loops.

EXTEND UNDERSTANDING Have children read the labels on the illustration on page 6. Ask: What do the lines that lead from each label tell you? Guide children to see how labels can be used to identify parts of an object.

RESPONSE OPTIONS

WRITING Have children describe what they might see or do on a space walk.

SCIENCE CONNECTION

Display books and other information about conditions in space. Have children work in pairs to make a chart that contrasts conditions in space and conditions on Earth.

Skill Work

TEACH/REVIEW VOCABULARY

Distribute sets of vocabulary word cards. Give clues to the words, such as "the opposite of play." Ask children to show the vocabulary word that goes with each clue.

TARGET SKILL AND STRATEGY

MAIN IDEA Tell children that a *topic* tells what a paragraph or article is about. The *main idea* is the most important idea about the topic. Sometimes the main idea is not given and children must state the main idea in their own words. Model using page 6: The topic of this paragraph is spacesuits. I think so because all the sentences are about spacesuits. I think the main idea is *A spacesuit helps an astronaut solve many space walk problems* because the details are examples of the problems that spacesuits solve.

TEXT STRUCTURE Remind children that *text structure* is the way information is organized. Explain that sometimes information is organized by the order in which it happens. Have children identify the order in which an astronaut performs a space walk.

ADDITIONAL SKILL INSTRUCTION

CAUSE AND EFFECT Remind children that as they read, they should think about *effects* (things that happen) and *causes* (why those things happen). Tell children that clue words such as *because, so, if, then,* and *since* often signal a cause-and-effect relationship. Give an example: "I hurt myself, *so* I cried." What happened is that I cried. The reason it happened is because I was hurt. Model questions children should ask as they read: After reading page 8, ask, What happened? *(An astronaut moves right, left, up, and down.)* Why did it happen? *(A special pack has rockets that help the astronaut move.)* Have children use a graphic organizer to keep track of causes and effects they read about.

Name _____

Main Idea

Read the passage below.
Fill in the topic, the main idea, and two supporting details.

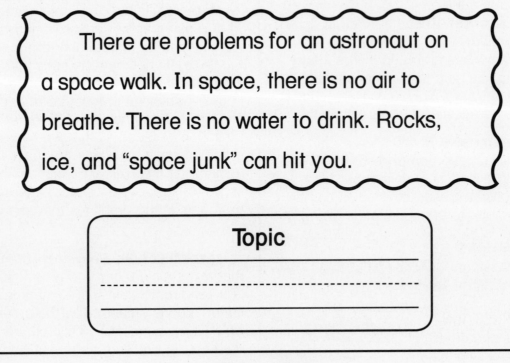

There are problems for an astronaut on a space walk. In space, there is no air to breathe. There is no water to drink. Rocks, ice, and "space junk" can hit you.

Topic
_____
_ _ _ _ _ _ _ _ _ _ _ _ _ _ _ _ _ _
_____

Main Idea
_____
_ _ _ _ _ _ _ _ _ _ _ _ _ _ _ _ _ _
_____

Supporting Details

_____	_____
_ _ _ _ _ _ _	_ _ _ _ _ _ _
_____	_____
_ _ _ _ _ _ _	_ _ _ _ _ _ _
_____	_____

Name _____

Vocabulary

Write a word from the box to answer each riddle.

Words to Know
everywhere   live   machines   move
woman   work   world

1. Some people travel around this. _____

2. Your work will be easier with these to help.

   _____

   _____

3. If I am your mother, I must be this. _____

4. Food, air, and water will help you do this. _____

5. Don't do this if you want to hide. _____

6. We can't be here at the same time.

   _____

   _____

7. You must do this to do a good job. _____

Camping at Crescent Lake

SUMMARY In this story, a family prepares for a camping trip. The story extends the lesson concept of what we can discover by exploring nature.

LESSON VOCABULARY

bear	build
couldn't	father
love	mother
straight	

INTRODUCE THE BOOK

INTRODUCE THE TITLE AND AUTHOR Discuss with children the title and author of *Camping at Crescent Lake*. Explain that social studies includes studying people's connection to nature. Ask: How might this book relate to social studies?

BUILD BACKGROUND Ask children to share what they know about camping. Ask: What kinds of things do people use when they go camping?

ELL Use maps and pictures of camping areas to help children understand what camping is all about.

PREVIEW/USE ILLUSTRATIONS Have children look at the pictures in the book before reading. Ask: What is this story about? Have children look at the heading, photo, and caption for the background information on page 12. Ask: What is this part of the book about?

READ THE BOOK

SET PURPOSE Have children set a purpose for reading *Camping at Crescent Lake*. Remind children of the characters they saw in their preview. Ask: What do you want to find out by reading this book?

STRATEGY SUPPORT: STORY STRUCTURE Remind children that good readers notice the structure of a story as they read—what happens at the beginning, middle, and end of the story. Remind them to think about the story's events as they read and how the story changes as it progresses.

COMPREHENSION QUESTIONS

PAGE 3 Which character trait best describes Jean: boy, old, or happy? *(happy)*

PAGES 4–6 Who had the best idea for where to camp? Why? *(Possible response: Father—he picked a place that Jean and Richard could both enjoy.)*

PAGE 6 What is a trail? *(Possible response: a path in the forest)*

PAGE 8 Where did the family put all the things they had packed? *(the kitchen)*

PAGE 10 Which way did the family drive first, next, and last? *(left, right, straight)*

REVISIT THE BOOK

THINK AND SHARE

1. The settings are the family's home and Crescent Lake. One is indoors and the other is outdoors.

2. Beginning: The family decided to go to Crescent Lake; Middle: The family planned and prepared for the trip; End: The family drove to Crescent Lake and enjoyed being there.

3. *str-:* straight, stream; *pl-:* explore, play, please, plan

4. Possible response: The answer is "Yes," since everyone seemed happy when they arrived at Crescent Lake.

EXTEND UNDERSTANDING Have children think about the theme of this story. Ask: What is the family in this story like? What do they do together? What do they do for each other? Guide children to see the theme of working together for the benefit of everyone.

RESPONSE OPTIONS

WRITING Have children write three sentences that describe what the family might see and do at Crescent Lake.

ART CONNECTION

Point out the three brochures in the story. Display a variety of real travel brochures. Have pairs of children each design a brochure for a local nature destination.

Skill Work

TEACH/REVIEW VOCABULARY

Write this story on the board without the underlined words, and have children use vocabulary words to complete the sentences: <u>Father</u> *will* <u>build</u> *a campfire. The boy and girl* <u>couldn't</u> *find many* <u>straight</u> *sticks.* <u>Mother</u> *said, "Crooked ones are fine. We just need to make a big fire to keep away a* <u>bear</u> *that would* <u>love</u> *to snack on our food."*

TARGET SKILL AND STRATEGY

⊚ CHARACTER AND SETTING *Characters* are the people or animals in stories. Authors describe their characters' traits—what the characters look like, how they act, and what kind of people they are. As they read, have children describe each character. Next, tell children that the *setting* is the time and place of a story. Explain that a setting can be a real place or an imaginary one. After children have identified the main place, ask them to identify the season. As they read, have children tell how the setting changes in the story.

⊚ STORY STRUCTURE Remind children that the beginning, middle, and end of a story make up the *story structure*. As they read, have children tell what happens at the beginning, middle, and end of *Camping at Crescent Lake*.

ADDITIONAL SKILL INSTRUCTION

SEQUENCE Remind children that as they read, they should think about what happens first, next, and last. Explain that clue words like *after* and *at last* can help them figure out the order of events. Point out the word *finally* on page 10. Explain that this clue word tells us that the camping part of this story happened last. You may have children use a graphic organizer to keep track of the sequence of events as they read the story.

Name _____

Character and Setting

Read each sentence below.
Circle the answer that best completes each sentence.

1. In the beginning of the story, Mother wants to

   a. read the newspaper.   b. plan a trip.   c. go back to bed.

2. The family camped

   a. in the desert.   b. near the beach.   c. in the forest.

3. Father was

   a. helpful.   b. sad.   c. tired.

4. In the story, Mother

   a. drove the car.   b. read the map.   c. saw a bear.

5. Write three things that Jean liked.

_____

_____

_____

Name _____

Vocabulary

Draw a line to match each word on the left with the word or words on the right that mean the opposite.

1. build   **a.** hate

2. couldn't   **b.** mother

3. father   **c.** was able to

4. love   **d.** tear down

Write each word from the box to best complete the sentence.

Words to Know
bear   mother   straight

5. The little _____ cub walked

_____ up to Jean's

_____ .

Desert Animals

SUMMARY Children read interesting facts about animals that live in the desert.

LESSON VOCABULARY

animals	early
eyes	full
warm	water

INTRODUCE THE BOOK

INTRODUCE THE TITLE AND AUTHOR Discuss the title and author of *Desert Animals*. Based on the title and the illustration on the cover, ask children to describe what they think this book might be about. Ask children if they've ever seen a plant or animal that look like the ones on the cover, and tell where.

BUILD BACKGROUND Discuss what children know about the desert and the animals that might live there. Have children think about special features that animals living in the desert must have in order to survive.

PREVIEW/TAKE A PICTURE WALK Invite children to take a picture walk to preview the text and illustrations. Point out the special features some of the animals in this book have that might help them survive in the desert.

READ THE BOOK

SET PURPOSE Have children set a purpose for reading *Desert Animals*. The discussion of desert animals while previewing the book should guide this purpose.

STRATEGY SUPPORT: IMPORTANT IDEAS Tell children that they will read numerous ideas about a topic, but that some of the ideas will be more important than others. Point out that some ideas might be very interesting, but might not be as important as others or might not relate directly to the topic. Stress that important ideas all relate to the book's topic and tell specific information or facts about the topic. After reading page 4, ask: Which facts on this page are important? Which fact is not as important as the others? Lead children to understand that knowing a camel can drink 36 gallons of water in six minutes is very interesting, but it may not be as important as knowing that it only drinks once a week.

COMPREHENSION QUESTIONS

PAGES 3–4 What are the most important ideas on these pages? (*Desert animals can go a long time without water; camels drink once a week.*)

PAGES 5–6 When does a jack rabbit hunt for food? (*early evening*)

PAGES 7–9 What do a desert owl and a hawk have in common? (*They have good eyes to see at night and to find food.*)

PAGES 10–12 Which idea did you find most interesting on these pages? (*Possible response: That the desert's temperatures change so drastically.*) How important do you think this idea is, and why? (*Answers will vary.*)

REVISIT THE BOOK

THINK AND SHARE

1. Main idea: Animals can live and survive in a desert. Details: Some animals stay out of the sun and only come out at night when it's cool; some animals don't need much to drink; some animals have eyes that can see at night; some animals have big ears so they can hear other animals.

2. Possible response: I learned how much a camel can drink at one time. They can drink 35 gallons of water.

3. (page 6) Possible response: I do not like to get up *early* in the morning.

4. Possible response: Some animals can live in the desert because they have special features that help them survive in a hot, dry environment.

EXTEND UNDERSTANDING Explain to children that animals are not the only living things that can survive in the desert. Discuss plants and how their special structures help them survive. For example, cactuses do not need much water to survive.

RESPONSE OPTIONS

ART Have children "create" a new animal that can survive in the desert that has some of the features of the animals they read about in this book. Ask them to draw a picture of this new creature and write a caption that explains each of its "parts." For instance, "Its ears are big so it can hear its enemies approach."

SOCIAL STUDIES CONNECTION

Have children choose an interesting idea from *Desert Animals* that they would like to find out more about. For instance, suggest that they look on the Internet or in library reference books to see if they can find out how it is possible for a camel to hold so much water. Then ask them to report their findings to the rest of the class.

ELL Make sure children understand some of the words in the *Desert Animals* that they might not be familiar with, such as *gallons*, *burrows*, *flutters*, and *unfriendly*. Provide definitions for these words and have children practice saying the words and becoming familiar with their meanings.

Skill Work

TEACH/REVIEW VOCABULARY

Pair off children and ask them each to come up with a riddle for each vocabulary word. Have children take turns presenting the riddle and guessing the words. For instance, Partner A would say: I am the opposite of *late*. Partner B would answer, *early*. Then Partner B would provide a riddle for a different word, and Partner A would guess the word.

TARGET SKILL AND STRATEGY

MAIN IDEA Tell children that the *main idea* tells the most important thing about the topic. It's what all the facts and other ideas, or details, should tell about. Ask: After reading this book, what do you think it's all about? Help children understand the difference between the topic of a book and its main idea.

IMPORTANT IDEAS Remind children that the *details* are the little pieces of information that support the main idea, and that some ideas are more important than others. Ask: What is an important idea that you read? What is an idea that you read that is interesting, but maybe not so important?

ADDITIONAL SKILL INSTRUCTION

AUTHOR'S PURPOSE Point out to children that the *author's purpose* is the reason the author has for writing the book. Explain that authors often have more than one reason for writing. An author might write to persuade, to inform or explain, or to entertain. Ask: Why do you think the author wrote this book? Why do you think the author chose the animals she did for this book? Lead children to understand that the author's purpose for writing *Desert Animals* was to inform or explain.

Name_____

Main Idea

Write the main idea of *Desert Animals* in the center oval. Choose three animals from the book and write them in the smaller ovals. For each spoke, write an important idea about the animal.

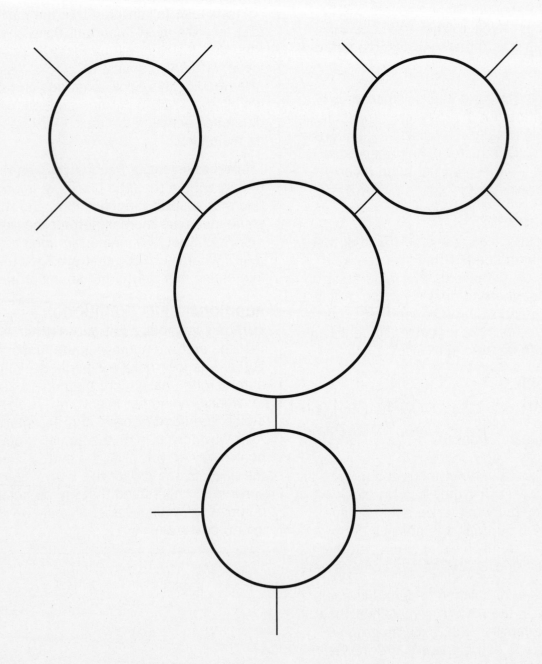

Name_____

Vocabulary

Write the word that best completes the sentence.

Words to Know
animals   early   eyes   full   warm   water

1. The desert is _____ of interesting animals.

2. The sun was so bright that I had to close my
_____.

3. We woke up extra _____ to get a head start!

4. Some plants don't need a lot of _____.

5. I love to go see the _____ at the zoo.

6. It was _____ outside, so we didn't bring
our jackets.

Glooskap and the First Summer

SUMMARY Children read a Native American myth about why the seasons change.

LESSON VOCABULARY

gone	learn	often
pieces	though	together
very		

INTRODUCE THE BOOK

INTRODUCE THE TITLE AND AUTHOR Discuss the title and author of *Glooskap and the First Summer: An Algonquin Tale*. Based on the title and the illustration on the cover, ask children to describe what they think this book might be about. Ask children why they think the cover illustration shows a man dressed in traditional Native American clothing.

BUILD BACKGROUND Discuss myths and folktales with children. Have children think about why people in the past might have written myths and folktales.

PREVIEW/TAKE A PICTURE WALK Invite children to take a picture walk to preview the text and illustrations. Discuss the different characters that Glooscap met as he traveled.

READ THE BOOK

SET PURPOSE Have children set a purpose for reading *Glooscap and the First Summer: An Algonquin Tale*. Ask them to think about how the different seasons are described in this myth.

STRATEGY SUPPORT: PREDICT AND SET PURPOSE Tell children that good readers set their purpose for reading by predicting what will probably happen next. Explain that they look for clues as they read to help them decide what might happen next in the story. Model questions to ask while reading: What is happening? Does this match what I predicted might happen? What changes could I make in my predictions?

COMPREHENSION QUESTIONS

PAGE 4 What facts about Winter are described in this text? *(It gets very cold. Plants died. Animals and people got hungry.)*

PAGE 5 What happens to Glooscap when he goes to see Winter? *(He falls asleep for months.)*

PAGE 8 What happens when Glooscap gets closer to Summer? *(It gets warm. There are flowers and trees.)*

PAGE 10 How is Summer's meeting with Winter like the seasons? *(As Summer gets closer, Winter starts to melt away.)*

REVISIT THE BOOK

THINK AND SHARE

1. Possible response: Fact: Seasons change; Details: Winter killed the plants; Winter put Glooksap to sleep; Summer melted Winter

2. Possible response: the seasons will change each year

3. Possible response: (page 3) If you often do something, that means you do it a lot.

4. Responses will vary, but children should understand the concept of myths and how they were created to explain things in nature.

EXTEND UNDERSTANDING Explain to children that many cultures have created stories like myths to tell the story of their people or explain things about the natural world. Discuss how the different characters tell you about the changing seasons. For example, Winter is a frozen old man who makes you want to go to sleep. The character of Summer is beautiful and can warm the icy Winter.

RESPONSE OPTIONS

ART Have children describe the things they like best about their favorite seasons. Have children draw a picture of their favorite season, name the different elements, and write a caption for the drawing.

DRAMA CONNECTION

Work with children to create a readers theater version of the story of Glooscap. Have children work in small groups to write dialogue for each character in the myth. Have groups take turns presenting the story of Glooscap with old man Winter, the Loon, the Whale, and Summer.

ELL Provide a T-chart for children. Have children label the columns *Summer* and *Winter*. Then have them write things about each season, including the name for each in their home language. Children can also draw pictures of the seasons.

Skill Work

TEACH/REVIEW VOCABULARY

Remind children that when they come to an unfamiliar word, they should look at its sentence and surrounding sentences for clues to its meaning. Direct children to find the word *together* on page 5. Ask a volunteer to explain its meaning. Ask what surrounding words or sentences gave clues to the meaning. Repeat for each vocabulary word.

TARGET SKILL AND STRATEGY

FACTS AND DETAILS Remind children that *facts* are pieces of information that can be proven to be true, and *details* are small pieces of information that support a fact. Give children a few sentences that present examples of facts and details. Have them identify the details and the information that supports the facts.

PREDICT AND SET PURPOSE Remind children that *predicting* is thinking about what will probably happen next. Ask children to discuss the predictions they made before reading *Glooscap and the First Summer: An Algonquin Tale*.

ADDITIONAL SKILL INSTRUCTION

DRAW CONCLUSIONS Remind children that *drawing conclusions* means thinking about facts and details and what you already know to make a decision about something. Direct children's attention to the text on page 11 and ask children to draw conclusions about what happened as Summer moved closer to Winter.

Name_____

Facts and Details

A **fact** is a piece of information that can be proven true.
Details are pieces of information about a story.

Read the following sentences.
Circle the the sentences that are details and underline the sentences that are facts.

1. Plant life changes in many ways in the winter cold.

2. Some plants die in winter snow.

3. Other plants called evergreens live through the winter.

4. Some plants just stop growing in winter.

5. These plants will sprout again in the spring.

6–7. Find two details that can be proven true from page 12.
Write them on the lines below.

_____

_____

_____

_____

_____

_____

_____

_____

Name_____

Vocabulary

Choose the word from the box that best completes each sentence.

Words to Know
gone   learn   often   pieces   though   together   very

1. Jack and Sam will _____ how to fish.

2. Mom _____ forgets to fill her gas tank.

3. My backpack was _____ from the shelf.

4. The vase broke into small _____ .

5. I will pack a swimsuit even _____ it might rain.

6. My new flute is _____ shiny.

7. Rico and I will get _____ to plan the party.

Be Ready for an Emergency

SUMMARY In this book, children learn how to prepare themselves for various kinds of emergencies. The sequence of events is emphasized through lists. Photographs build children's knowledge of what to expect in emergencies.

LESSON VOCABULARY

break	family
heard	listen
once	pull

INTRODUCE THE BOOK

INTRODUCE THE TITLE AND AUTHOR Discuss the title and the author of *Be Ready for an Emergency*. Ask children to describe what they see on the cover and how it relates to the title. Ask children what topics they think may be covered in this book.

BUILD BACKGROUND Discuss the types of situations that are emergencies. Ask children to name people in the community who help others during emergencies. (police officers, firefighters, and paramedics) Discuss school activities that prepare children for emergencies, such as fire drills.

ELL Invite children to pronounce content-related words, such as *emergency*, *firefighter*, *ambulance*, and *help*. Elicit class discussion about the similarities and differences between the emergency services of various cultures. Ask: Do you think there are firefighters and police officers all over the world?

PREVIEW/TAKE A PICTURE WALK Have children look at the photographs and the section headings throughout the book. Ask: How are the section headings similar? Do they give you clues as to what the book is about? How do the photographs relate to the headings?

READ THE BOOK

SET PURPOSE Thinking about potential emergencies may worry some children. Have them set a purpose for reading by looking for things they can do today to stay safe.

STRATEGY SUPPORT: SUMMARIZE To help children better understand how to *summarize*, discuss the concept of main ideas. Encourage students to talk about the rules they follow in school, and lead them to understand that the main idea of most of the rules is to be respectful— of their classmates, of school property, and of themselves. Remind them as they read *Be Ready for an Emergency*, to stop and think about the main rules they are being told.

COMPREHENSION QUESTIONS

PAGE 5 What happens when you call 9-1-1? *(You talk to someone who can send help.)*

PAGE 7 Why do you think you should do something different when you get lost inside than when you get lost outside? *(When you get lost inside there are adults nearby who can help you. When you are outside people may be farther away.)*

PAGE 8 Why should you not stop to take things with you? *(You must get out before the fire spreads.)*

PAGE 10 What kinds of things do you think the 9-1-1 operator will ask you if you are in an accident? *(Where are you? How many cars and people are in the accident? Is anyone hurt?)*

PAGE 12 How could you check yourself for injuries? *(I would look at where I felt pain to see if I was cut. I would also try to move my limbs.)*

REVISIT THE BOOK

THINK AND SHARE

1. Possible responses: Effect — You get hurt too. You can hurt the other person more.
2. Possible response: I learned ways to be prepared for an emergency.
3. Possible response: People may be calling for you.
4. Possible response: The adult would call for your parents over the loudspeaker.

EXTEND UNDERSTANDING When children come to pages 8 and 9, ask: How do the pictures help you understand why it is important to get away from a fire as fast as you can? Can you see why you should let the firefighters rescue people and pets who may be inside? Have children describe the firefighter's special clothes and equipment in the photograph on page 9. Lead them to conclude that firefighters are specially prepared to rescue people from fires.

RESPONSE OPTIONS

WRITING Have children write three things they can do to prepare for emergencies.

SOCIAL STUDIES CONNECTION

Many community fire departments have educational programs on fire safety for children. Arrange a class trip to a fire station, or have a firefighter visit your school.

Skill Work

TEACH/REVIEW VOCABULARY

Remind children that when they come to an unfamiliar word, they should look at its sentence and surrounding sentences for clues to its meaning. Direct children to find the word *heard* on page 10. Ask a volunteer to explain its meaning. Ask what surrounding words or sentences gave clues to the meaning. Repeat for each vocabulary word.

TARGET SKILL AND STRATEGY

CAUSE AND EFFECT Review with children that one event often causes another event to happen. As they read, challenge students to think about what happens (*effect*) and about why it happened (*cause*). For example, on page 7, the *effect* (what happens) is that people find you outdoors. The *cause*, or why it happened, is because you knew to stay in one spot when you are lost.

SUMMARIZE Remind children that being able to retell the main ideas of a book is a good way to show they understood what was happening as they read. Have children flip through the illustrations and use them to tell you only what they think are the most important rules during an emergency.

ADDITIONAL SKILL INSTRUCTION

MAIN IDEA Model how to identify the *main idea* on page 6. Begin by identifying the topic of the page—getting lost. Next, read each sentence aloud. Ask which sentence is the most important of the three. Have children explain the topic and main idea on page 8. Ask volunteers to share their answers.

Name_____

Cause and Effect

Write the missing **cause** or **effect**.
Use *Be Ready for an Emergency* to help you.

1. **CAUSE:** You are lost indoors.

   _____

   EFFECT: _____

2. **CAUSE:** _____

   EFFECT: The air is easier to breathe down by the floor.

3. **CAUSE:** There is no other way out of the house.

   _____

   EFFECT: _____

4. **CAUSE:** _____

   EFFECT: The operator tells you what to do.

5. **CAUSE:** You read *Be Ready for an Emergency*.

   _____

   EFFECT: _____

Name_____

Vocabulary

Draw a line to match each word to its meaning.

Words to Know
break   family   heard   listen   once   pull

1. break

a. people who are related to each other

2. family

b. received sounds through the ear

3. heard

c. a single time

4. listen

d. to hurt or damage

5. once

e. to pay attention to sounds

6. pull

f. to move by dragging or tugging

7. Write a sentence using a vocabulary word from the box.

_____

_____

_____

Let's Work Together!

SUMMARY In this fiction selection, Simon and his friends want to plant flowers at their playground, but they can't agree on a way to raise money. The friends argue. They can't find a way to work together until Simon's dad gives Simon some good advice to share with his friends.

LESSON VOCABULARY

certainly	either
great	laugh
second	worst
you're	

INTRODUCE THE BOOK

INTRODUCE THE TITLE AND AUTHOR Discuss the title and author of *Let's Work Together!* Have children look at the cover and ask how the picture relates to the title. Ask them why they think the author wanted to write a book about working together.

BUILD BACKGROUND Talk to children about times that they have worked together with friends or classmates. Discuss the reason they worked together. Talk about any problems that came up during the project and how those problems were solved.

ELL Invite children to pronounce *playground*, *flowers*, *tools*, *argument*, *plan*, *car*, *yard*, and *toy* in English. Encourage them to tell about similarities or differences between another neighborhood they may know and their new neighborhood.

PREVIEW/TAKE A PICTURE WALK Have children look through the book at the illustrations. Guide them to get to know the characters by studying the illustrations. Ask: What kinds of feelings are the characters showing in each picture?

READ THE BOOK

SET PURPOSE Have children set a purpose for reading by looking at the cover illustration. Ask children to predict why the children are raking leaves. Guide children to read to find out whether their predictions are correct.

STRATEGY SUPPORT: STORY STRUCTURE Tell children that good readers notice the *story structure*, or the beginning, middle, and end of a story, as they read. Remind them to think about the story's events as they read and how the story changes with each event that occurs.

COMPREHENSION QUESTIONS

PAGE 3 Where did the children want to plant flowers? *(at the playground)*

PAGE 7 Who helped Simon come up with a solution to the children's problem? *(Simon's dad)*

PAGE 10 How did the children solve their problem? *(They decided to do yard work first, sell used toys or games second, and then wash cars.)*

PAGE 11 Does the author approve or disapprove of working together? How do you know? *(He approves. The children enjoy working together in the end.)*

REVISIT THE BOOK

THINK AND SHARE

1. Possible response: to entertain and to teach a lesson about working together to end a disagreement.
2. Possible response: They all wanted to raise money, but they didn't agree on how to raise it. At the end of the story, they all agree on how to raise money. They are happy to work together.
3. We'll be happy to go; She's doing her homework; Don't forget your bag; I'm going to the store.
4. They learned that they could make a plan to make everyone happy. They also learned that it was fun to work together.

EXTEND UNDERSTANDING Remind children that they can usually tell the main idea of a book in one sentence. Ask children to think about the main idea of this book. Ask them to say it in one sentence.

RESPONSE OPTIONS

WRITING Ask children to write two sentences about a favorite character from the story.

SOCIAL STUDIES CONNECTION

Time For
SOCIAL
STUDIES

Discuss with children an area of the school or neighborhood that needs improvement. Have small groups create a mock plan to raise money for the improvement.

Skill Work

TEACH/REVIEW VOCABULARY

Have children complete sentences using vocabulary words. Write a sentence on the board for each vocabulary word, such as: *She will _____ at my "knock, knock" jokes. (laugh)* Next to the sentences, in a different order, write the vocabulary words. Ask volunteers to choose the correct words and write them on the lines.

TARGET SKILL AND STRATEGY

AUTHOR'S PURPOSE Remind children that an author usually has a purpose for writing. Prompt them to think about the *author's purpose* while reading. This will help them set their own purpose for reading.

STORY STRUCTURE Remind children that the beginning, middle, and end of a story make up the *story structure*. As they read, have children tell what happens at the beginning, middle, and end of *Let's Work Together!*

ADDITIONAL SKILL INSTRUCTION

CHARACTER, SETTING, PLOT Review with children that the *characters* are people or animals in the story, and *setting* is where and when the story takes place. The events that occur and the problems that arise make up the *plot*. Have children identify the main characters. *(Simon, Anna, Mike, Mary, Simon's dad)* Have children identify the setting at the end of the story. *(the playground)* Ask children to identify the important events of the story and how Simon felt at different points.

Name _____

Author's Purpose

Read the text below. Then circle the best answer for each question.

> Simon started a list. "First we'll do yard work," he said.
> "The second week we'll sell used toys or games," said Anna.
> "Then we'll wash cars," said Mary.
> "That's a great plan!" said Mike.

1. Why did the author write about Simon and his friends making a plan?
   a. to teach
   b. to be funny
   c. to be sad

2. What is another reason the author wrote about Simon and his friends?
   a. so that you will like the author
   b. so that you will do yard work
   c. so that you will have a good story to read

3. How does the author want you to feel about making plans with friends?
   a. that it is too hard
   b. that it is a bad idea
   c. that it can be fun

4. Write a sentence that tells what you think about making plans with friends after reading *Let's Work Together!*

   _____
   _____
   _____

Name _____

Vocabulary

Draw a line to match the word to its meaning.

Words to Know
certainly   either   great   laugh
second   worst   you're

1. certainly   a. one of two things

2. either   b. surely

3. great   c. a sound made by someone when something is funny

4. laugh   d. you are

5. second   e. the next after first

6. you're   f. very good

Antonyms are words that have opposite meanings. Draw a line from the word to its antonym.

7. either   g. best

8. great   h. terrible

9. laugh   i. both

10. worst   j. cry

Farming Families

SUMMARY Anna's family lives on a farm. The whole family works hard to take care of their orange trees. Anna and her brothers work on the farm after school. In October, the family harvests their oranges. Then they sell the oranges to stores.

LESSON VOCABULARY

above	ago	enough
toward	whole	word

INTRODUCE THE BOOK

INTRODUCE THE TITLE AND AUTHOR Discuss with children the title and the author of *Farming Families*. Then have children look at the cover. Explain that science includes the topic of how plants and trees grow. Ask: How might this book relate to science?

BUILD BACKGROUND Have children discuss what they know about farms. Ask them to share anything they know about the foods farmers grow.

PREVIEW/TAKE A PICTURE WALK Have children look at the pictures in the book before reading. Ask: What food is Anna's family growing? Does it grow in the ground or on trees? How do you know?

ELL Show children pictures to help them identify the words *store, farm, orange, tree, sun* and *rain*. This will help them understand the text by connecting a familiar image to an English word.

READ THE BOOK

SET PURPOSE Have children set a purpose for reading *Farming Families*. Remind children of what they discussed about farms and the foods that grow on farms. Ask: What do you want to learn about farming?

STRATEGY SUPPORT: BACKGROUND KNOWLEDGE As children finish reading page 5, pause and model how to connect the text to their background knowledge. Say: This reminds me of a dairy farm I visited. Instead of working together to take care of orange trees, the family worked together to take care of the cows. Has anybody else ever visited a farm? What do you know about farms? Pause again after reading page 11, and ask children if they have had an experience similar to Anna's. If necessary, connect harvest time with doing chores or spring cleaning.

COMPREHENSION QUESTIONS

PAGE 4 Where does some food that we buy in stores come from? *(farms)*

PAGE 7 What do oranges need to grow? *(sun and rain)*

PAGE 8 Why do you think the author wrote this page? *(to let us know what happens at harvest time)*

PAGE 10 What do you think it would be like to work on a farm during harvest time? *(Responses will vary but should reflect the understanding that farm families work hard for long hours during harvest time.)*

REVISIT THE BOOK

THINK AND SHARE

1. Oranges need sun, rain, and orange trees need trimming to grow.
2. Responses will vary but should be knowledge they had prior to reading pages 10 and 11.
3. Oranges grow above the ground. The whole family works hard on the farm. The family has enough oranges to feed other people.
4. Responses will vary.

EXTEND UNDERSTANDING Have children examine the pictures. Ask: What do you see in the pictures that is not explained in words? Guide children to see how the pictures add to their understanding of families living and working together on a farm.

RESPONSE OPTIONS

WRITING Have children write two or three sentences about whether or not they would like to live and work on a farm with their family.

SCIENCE CONNECTION

TIME FOR Science

Using the Internet, have children do guided research on orange trees. Have them find out where they grow, how long it takes for them to grow, and the type of care they need.

Skill Work

TEACH/REVIEW VOCABULARY

Write this story on the board: A while _after_, I needed a special coin to make my collection _half._ I finally saved a _little_ money, so I biked _away from_ the mall. I went to the store that had a sign _below_ the door with the _number_ Coins. Have children replace the underlined words with vocabulary words so that the story makes sense.

TARGET SKILL AND STRATEGY

FACTS AND DETAILS Explain to children that a _fact_ is a bit of information that can be proven true. _Details_ are pieces of information that help you picture what you need. The main idea of this story is that farming families must work hard for their harvest. Details such as a description of the work that must be completed help explain this idea. So do facts—details that can be proven to be true—such as what orange trees need to grow. Ask children to find three details in the book and read them aloud.

BACKGROUND KNOWLEDGE TTell children that they can use what they already know to help them understand what they read. Have children use a KWL chart for _Farming Families_ to generate questions for which they will look for answers as they read.

ADDITIONAL SKILL INSTRUCTION

CAUSE AND EFFECT Remind children, as they read, to think about things that happen and why those things happen. Model questions children should ask as they read. After reading page 11, ask: _What happened? Why did it happen?_ Invite children to use a cause-and-effect graphic organizer as they read.

Name _____

Facts and Details

A **fact** is a piece of information that can be proven true.
Details are pieces of information about a story.

Read the details. Circle the details and underline facts that you find
in the following sentences from *Farming Families*.

1. Most people today buy their food in stores.

2. Anna's family owns an orange farm.

3. It is too much work for most people to own a farm.

4. Anna's big brothers pick fruit that is high above her head.

5. It feels good to rest after the harvest.

_____

6–7. Find two details that can be proven true from *Farm Families*.
Write them on the lines below.

_____
- -
_____
_____
- -
_____
_____
- -
_____
_____
- -
_____

Name _____

Vocabulary

Use words from the box to complete the paragraph.

Words to Know		
above	ago	enough
toward	whole	word

_____

Long _____, almost every family was a _____

farming family. They had to grow _____

food to last all year. They spent the _____

day working on the farm. Some fruit grew high _____

_____ their heads. They started to feel _____

tired _____ the end of the harvest.

Now write a sentence using one or more words from the box.

_____

_____

_____

_____

_____

Growing Up

SUMMARY This story shows similarities between how a dog and a boy grow up. Jun, who is afraid of dogs, learns that a dog can be a friend. The selection supports and extends the concept of working together.

LESSON VOCABULARY

bought	people
pleasant	probably
scared	shall
sign	

INTRODUCE THE BOOK

INTRODUCE THE TITLE AND AUTHOR Discuss the title and the author of *Growing Up*. Invite children to comment on the the cover illustrations and how they relate to the title. Encourage children to predict how the book may relate to science.

BUILD BACKGROUND Compare the stages of both animal and human development. Ask: What are some of the first things a baby learns? What are some of the first things a puppy learns? What do you need to know when you start school? What do you learn in school? What are some of the things people train a dog to do? At what age do you think a puppy becomes an adult dog?

PREVIEW/TAKE A PICTURE WALK Remind children to browse the book before reading and to look at the pictures. Prompt children to predict what the book will be about. Ask: What do the labels with the illustrations tell you? How old are Jun and Pepper in the beginning of the book? How old are they at the end of the book?

READ THE BOOK

SET PURPOSE Model how to set a purpose for reading by looking at the title and the cover. Say: I think this book will be about a boy and his dog. I want to find out what it is like to have a dog and how to take care of it. I will read to find out. Then ask: What do you want to learn in this story? Remind children to think about what they want to learn as they read.

STRATEGY SUPPORT: STORY STRUCTURE Remind children that good readers notice the structure of a story as they read—what happens at the beginning, middle, and end of the story. Remind them to think about the story's events as they read and how the story changes as it progresses.

COMPREHENSION QUESTIONS

PAGE 3 Who is Soo Mi? *(Jun's sister)*

PAGE 4 What didn't Jun like about Pepper? *(Pepper jumped on Jun.)*

PAGE 6 Why did the author tell you about Jun and Pepper going to school? *(to show the similarities between them)*

PAGE 9 What does the fact that Pepper ran to Jun tell you? *(Possible response: Pepper is loyal to Jun.)*

PAGE 10 When Pepper was sick, he was taken to the vet. When Jun is sick, where does he go? *(to the doctor)*

REVISIT THE BOOK

THINK AND SHARE

1. Jun said that Pepper keeps sneezing. They took him to the vet. She took a bug out of Pepper's nose.
2. Possible response: At first he was scared of Pepper, and at the end he was very fond of Pepper.
3. Possible responses: paws: The dog put his front paws on Jun; boxes: Jun hid behind the boxes; puppies: Puppies grow up faster than children.
4. Possible response: I would like to have fish, because they are colorful.

EXTEND UNDERSTANDING After reading, simplify the concept of theme by describing it as the big idea of the story. Lead children to identify the story's theme by revisiting the earlier discussion about the author's purpose. Ask: What does the author want to express through the story of Jun and Pepper?

RESPONSE OPTIONS

WRITING Have children write a sentence describing one thing they have in common with Jun.

ELL Have children complete a simple Venn Diagram. Tell them to write three facts comparing and contrasting the events of Jun and Pepper growing up.

SCIENCE CONNECTION

Ask children to go to the library and pick out a book about their favorite animal. Ask them to present to the class one similarity and one difference between themselves and the young of their favorite animal.

Skill Work

TEACH/REVIEW VOCABULARY

Lead a synonym activity. First, describe synonyms as words with the same meaning. Group children in pairs and assign each pair a vocabulary word and its synonym: *people/ humans, sign/signal, shall/will, bought/ purchased, pleasant/nice, scared/frightened.* Have pairs write a sentence that uses their word's synonym, and then read their sentences to the group. Then ask the group to replace the synonym with the vocabulary word.

TARGET SKILL AND STRATEGY

CAUSE AND EFFECT As they read, remind children to think about things that happen *(effects)* and why those things happen *(causes).* Remind them that often in a story one event causes another event to take place. Model questions to ask after reading page 3: What happened? Dad brought home a puppy, but Jun didn't like him. Why? He didn't like Pepper jumping up on him. Have children use a cause-and-effect chart to keep track of what happened and why it happened.

STORY STRUCTURE Noticing the *story structure* can help children better understand what they read. Ask children what happened at the beginning, middle, and end of the story. Write each event on a piece of paper. Have children put the pieces of paper in the correct order of the story's events.

ADDITIONAL SKILL INSTRUCTION

CHARACTER, SETTING, AND PLOT Review basic literary elements such as setting, character, and plot by asking children simple questions. Prompt them to think about the story's setting. Ask: Where did the story take place? When did the story take place? Prompt children to think about the characters by asking them who the people and animals in the story are and what they know about them. Lead children to think about plot by asking them what happened in the beginning, middle, and end of the story.

Name _____

Cause and Effect

Fill in the numbered boxes to tell what happened (effect) or why it happened (cause).

Why did it happen? (Cause) **What happened? (Effect)**

Jun ran into the basement.	→	1.

2.	→	Jun knew Pepper liked him.

3.	→	Pepper learned not to jump up on people.

Pepper sneezed all day.	→	4.

Jun said that he and Pepper will always be friends.	→	5.

Name _____

Vocabulary

Use a word from the box to complete each sentence.

Words to Know			
bought	people	pleasant	probably
scared	shall	sign	

_____

1. Dad _____ a puppy and took it home.

_____

2. Jun was _____ when dogs jumped on him.

_____

3. Dad though Jun would _____ get used
   to Pepper.

_____

4. Pepper learned not to jump up on _____.

_____

5. Pepper's tongue felt rough to Jun, but _____.

_____

6. _____ we take Pepper to the park?

_____

7. When Pepper licked Jun, it was a _____ that
   Pepper liked him.

Showing Good Manners

SUMMARY This instructional text uses fictional characters to illustrate how having good manners is important in getting along with others. A teacher and four students demonstrate six good manners that help them to be good friends.

LESSON VOCABULARY

behind	brought
door	everybody
minute	promise
sorry	

INTRODUCE THE BOOK

INTRODUCE THE TITLE AND AUTHOR Discuss with children the title and author of *Getting Along*. Based on the title, ask children what kind of information they think this book will provide. Does the cover illustration give any additional clues?

BUILD BACKGROUND Ask children to talk about how they get along with their friends and family members. Ask: What advice would you give about how to get along with classmates? family members? What are some ways that have helped you get along with others? What are some things that people should NOT do if they want to get along with one another?

ELL Ask children to share the words for *please*, *thank you*, and *excuse me* in other languages they may know. Discuss other words they know that show good manners, and talk about when those words might be used.

PREVIEW/TAKE A PICTURE WALK Invite children to look at the pictures in the book. Then ask them how the pictures give clues to what the book will be about.

READ THE BOOK

SET PURPOSE Have children set a purpose for reading *Getting Along*. As they read, have children think about a time when they were not able to get along with someone. Ask them to think about how this book might have been helpful at that time.

STRATEGY SUPPORT: INFERRING Explain to children that *inferring* is taking information you read in a story and making a guess about something the author didn't mention. You can infer things from the illustrations and also from the characters' actions. Encourage students to make inferences as they read the story.

COMPREHENSION QUESTIONS

PAGES 6–7 Look at the picture of Nikki on page 6. How does she look? *(sad, hurt)* Look at the picture of Nikki on page 7. How does she look? *(happy)*

PAGE 7 What caused Nikki to smile in this picture? *(Marco and Maggie are using good manners and are listening to Nikki.)*

PAGE 10 What is another way Maggie can show good manners after she has broken Alex's pencil? *(She can offer Alex a new pencil.)*

PAGE 12 Why should we all try to show good manners? *(Good manners help us get along with others and be good friends.)*

REVISIT THE BOOK

THINK AND SHARE

1. Good Manners: I would pick the books up and say "I'm sorry." Bad Manners: I would walk away without helping. Good Manners: I would wait my turn in line. Bad Manners: I would cut in front of the person in line. Good Manners: I would wait quietly for them to finish talking. Bad Manners: I would start talking while my mom is talking.

2. Possible responses: Nikki is helpful and happy to help. Marco studies hard or likes to read books.

3. Words with long *a*: waiting, today, breaking, say, take; sentences will vary.

4. Responses will vary.

EXTEND UNDERSTANDING Point out to children that although this book is presented with fictional characters, the setting and the school situations are realistic. Discuss with them how the lessons in the book could be helpful in their own school.

RESPONSE OPTIONS

WRITING Ask children to visualize a scene in which two classmates are using good manners. In a few sentences, have them write down what the classmates say and do, how they look, and how they feel.

SOCIAL STUDIES CONNECTION

Time For SOCIAL STUDIES

First, brainstorm with children a situation in the classroom in which they would be working in groups. Then, have them write a list of good manners that would help them achieve the goal of getting along with each other. Encourage children to brainstorm good manners that are not already listed in the book.

Skill Work

TEACH/REVIEW VOCABULARY

Go over the meaning of the vocabulary words. Tell children you have chosen a mystery word, and it is their job to guess what the word is, based on three clues about the word. Create clues for all vocabulary words.

TARGET SKILL AND STRATEGY

COMPARE AND CONTRAST Tell children that to *compare and contrast* is to look for how things are the same and how they are different. During reading, have children compare and contrast good manners and bad manners in each situation described.

INFERRING Remind children that *inferring* is when you make a guess about the story or a character without being told that information by the author. Read page 5 with the class and then ask: What can you infer that Nikki is talking about during her Show and Tell? How do you know this?

ADDITIONAL SKILL INSTRUCTION

CAUSE AND EFFECT Remind children that an *effect* is what happened and a *cause* is why something happened. As children read the text, have them think about the effects of good manners and bad manners. For example, after reading page 8, ask: What happened when Alex kept his promise to Maggie? Why do you think Alex decided to keep his promise and play kickball?

Name _____

Compare and Contrast

You learned about good manners and bad manners in the book *Showing Good Manners.* Compare and contrast the good and bad manners that can help us get along or not. Use manners you read about in the book, as well as manners that were not in the text. Use the Venn diagram below to help organize your information.

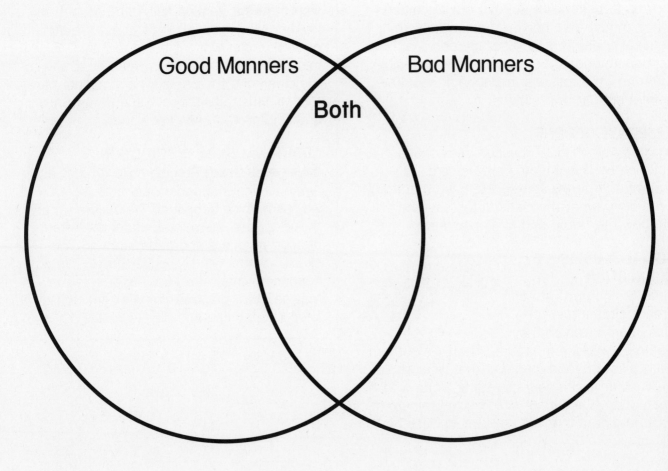

Good Manners

Both

Bad Manners

Name _____

Vocabulary

Draw a line from each word to its meaning.

Words to Know
behind   brought   door   everybody
minute   promise   sorry

1. behind

2. brought

3. door

4. everybody

5. minute

6. promise

7. sorry

a. each and every person

b. at the back of

c. feeling sadness or regret

d. to give your word

e. the entrance of a building or room that opens and closes

f. carried or taken with you

g. 60 seconds

8. Write a sentence using at least one word from the box.

_____

_____

_____

_____

Dotty's Art

SUMMARY Dotty worries that she can't draw, but she follows her dad's suggestion and comes up with her very own way of making art. After working all week to make a special picture, she wins a prize at the school art show.

LESSON VOCABULARY

guess	pretty	science
shoe	village	watch
won		

INTRODUCE THE BOOK

INTRODUCE THE TITLE AND AUTHOR Discuss with children the title and the author of *Dotty's Art*. Draw children's attention to the cover illustration. Ask: What do you think this story will be about? Have you ever read any other books about art?

BUILD BACKGROUND Ask children if they like to make art or if they have ever seen art that they enjoy. Using the Internet, reference books, postcards, or other sources, show children reproductions of art. Discuss different media that artists use to create, such as clay, wood, stone, watercolor paints, colored pencils, magazine clippings, and everyday objects.

PREVIEW/USE ILLUSTRATIONS Have children read the title and look carefully at the illustrations. Discuss what these suggest about the story's content and possible ending. Look, for example, at the illustration on page 11 and ask: Why do you think Dotty is holding a blue ribbon? Do you think the ending of this story will be happy?

READ THE BOOK

SET PURPOSE Guide children to set their own purposes for reading the selection. Children's interest in art should guide this purpose. Suggest that children imagine an art project that they enjoyed making or that they might enjoy creating.

STRATEGY SUPPORT: QUESTIONING Explain to children that there is more than one way to find answers to questions. Some answers can be found right in the book. For other questions, they may need to use what they already know to find the answer to a question. Point out question 1 in Think and Share and ask them how they would find the answer.

COMPREHENSION QUESTIONS

PAGE 3 What was the first event in this story? *(Mr. Dean explained that each student could enter a piece of art in the school art show.)*

PAGE 4 What was Dotty's first response when she heard about the art show? *(She worried because she had no idea for a project.)*

PAGE 8 How did Dotty's feelings change after she finished making her art? *(She wasn't worried anymore; she liked her art and called it pretty.)*

PAGES 10–11 What do you think the author feels about the fact that Dotty won a prize? How do you know? *(It was a happy event; the author used exclamation points.)*

REVISIT THE BOOK

THINK AND SHARE

1. Possible responses: She wanted children to know that if they really think about a problem, they can come up with a solution. She also wanted to tell us about an interesting way to make a picture.
2. Responses will vary but should include a question and answer showing they understand the story.
3. Answers will vary but should include a description of their experience.
4. Possible responses: They had been to an art show. They knew about a famous painter.

EXTEND UNDERSTANDING Explain to children that fictional stories often have *themes*, or big ideas, that convey a general truth or opinion. Help children find the theme of *Dotty's Art*— that there are all kinds of ways to make art, and making art is fun. After discussing the theme, ask them to use their own words to state it in a way that makes sense to them.

RESPONSE OPTIONS

VIEWING Bring in examples from books, magazines, or the Internet of many different kinds of art. If possible, include a pointillist painting by Seurat, such as *A Sunday Afternoon on La Grande Jatte*. After children have seen images by different artists, have them discuss which images they like and why.

ART CONNECTION

Have children create their own art exhibition, with each child contributing one piece of art. Encourage children to use whatever materials are on hand, such as pencils, crayons, or clay. Invite them to use nontraditional materials also, such as leaves or cellophane wrappers. Ask each child to give his or her work a title.

Skill Work

TEACH/REVIEW VOCABULARY

In one column on the board, write short definitions of the vocabulary words. In another column, write a list of the words. Invite children to come up one at a time and draw a colored line connecting a definition to the correct word, until all the definitions are linked to their words.

ELL Distribute vocabulary word cards and invite children to go on a scavenger hunt looking for the same word in other classroom books or written materials.

TARGET SKILL AND STRATEGY

AUTHOR'S PURPOSE Remind children that an author has a reason or reasons for writing. An author might wish, for example, to give information or make readers laugh. As children read, invite them to speculate about why the author wrote *Dotty's Art*. Guide children to look for clues in the text, such as Dotty's actions or feelings.

QUESTIONING Explain that good readers know how to ask questions about what they read. Ask: What suggestion did Dotty's Dad give her? Can anyone name another "dot artist" besides Dotty? Have children create their own questions.

ADDITIONAL SKILL INSTRUCTION

SEQUENCE Remind children that one event follows another in most stories. Explain that this is called the *sequence* of events. Help them to keep track of what happens first, next, and last. On the board, write down this story's clue words, such as *after* and *finally*, and suggest that children look for these as they read.

Name _____

Author's Purpose

Read these paragraphs. Then answer the questions.

> Dotty took crayons, markers, and a giant piece of paper. She started dotting away. She made big dots, little dots, and dots of every color. She filled her paper with thousands of dots. It took all week.
>
> Finally, she finished. There was a little dot village, little dot bees and fleas, and little dot people eating dot peas. One dot even wore a little dot shoe.

1. Why do you think the author wrote the first paragraph?

_____

- -

_____

2. Explain your answer.

_____

- -

_____

- -

_____

3. Why do you think the author wrote the second paragraph?

_____

- -

_____

4. Explain your answer.

_____

- -

_____

- -

_____

Name _____

Vocabulary

Write a word from the box to complete each sentence.

Words to Know			
guess	pretty	science	shoe
village	watch	won	

1. Dotty had art after her _____ class.

2. Dotty made a picture of a little dot _____ .

3. One dot person wore a little dot _____ .

4. At the exhibit, Dotty liked to _____ people looking at her dots.

5. Can you _____ what you would draw for an exhibit?

6. Dotty liked Maria's _____ clay turtle.

7. In the end, Dotty _____ a blue ribbon.

Living in Seoul

SUMMARY A girl named Mina tells about her life in Seoul, South Korea. She tells about the climate, her family, children's games, school, famous places, and holidays.

LESSON VOCABULARY

answer company

faraway parents

picture school

wash

INTRODUCE THE BOOK

INTRODUCE THE TITLE AND AUTHOR Discuss with children the title and the author of *Living in Seoul*. Based on the title, ask children what kind of information they think this book will provide.

BUILD BACKGROUND Discuss what children know about Korea. Ask if they know what continent it is on. Help children find Korea on a globe or world map. Ask if they know anyone who comes from Korea or if they have any Korean relatives. Have children tell about their knowledge of Korea.

PREVIEW/TAKE A PICTURE WALK Invite children to look at the pictures in the selection. Start with the photograph on the title page. Ask children if they have seen a building like this before. Do they think this story will be about the area where they live? Ask them what they think they will learn.

READ THE BOOK

SET PURPOSE Have children set a purpose for reading *Living in Seoul*. Their interest in learning about children in other cultures should guide this purpose. Suggest that children plan to write a letter telling about their own lives in their town or city. Suggest they model their own stories on the story in this selection.

STRATEGY SUPPORT: VISUALIZE Tell children that good readers form pictures in their minds as they read. After reading page 4, ask children to close their eyes. Reread the page aloud to them. Ask them to form pictures in their minds as you read and then share with the class what they visualized.

COMPREHENSION QUESTIONS

PAGE 3 Where does Mina live? What kind of place is Seoul? *(Seoul, South Korea; a large city)*

PAGE 5 How many seasons does she tell about? What are they? *(3; summer, winter, rainy season)*

PAGE 7 What happens at the morning meeting? *(The principal shares important news; children bow and thank the principal.)*

PAGE 8 What do the children do after school? *(They stay and help clean up their own classroom—emptying trash, sweeping floors, and washing blackboards.)*

PAGE 12 What is Mina's favorite part of the New Year's Day celebration? *(flying kites)*

REVISIT THE BOOK

THINK AND SHARE

1. Possible responses: special events of the day, upcoming events, special achievements
2. Responses will vary, but should reflect an understanding that visualizing text can help increase understanding.
3. Answers will vary according to how well children know and understand the words.
4. Possible responses: Same—living with family, playing games with friends, going to school, listening to morning announcements, enjoying holidays; different—having school on Saturdays, visiting palaces, flying kites on New Year's Day

EXTEND UNDERSTANDING Have children look at a world map or globe. Invite them to point to the United States and to Korea. Ask children to discuss in pairs the location of these two countries. Ask: What continent is each located on? *(North America, Asia)* Ask them to talk about how close or far away the United States and Korea are from each other. Help them estimate distance using the scale of miles.

RESPONSE OPTIONS

WRITING Have children write stories about a child's life in their town or city. Suggest that they model their stories on the selection. Invite them to illustrate their stories. Make an exhibition of their books titled, "A Child's Life in [your town or city]."

SOCIAL STUDIES CONNECTION

Children can learn more about Korean holidays by doing guided research on the Internet or in the library. Suggest they find out what other holidays are important to Koreans and how these special days are celebrated.

Skill Work

TEACH/REVIEW VOCABULARY

To reinforce the meaning of *faraway*, read page 10. Talk about how the words on this page help explain the meaning of the word. Talk about what "come from faraway places" might mean for Mina. Ask them what "faraway places" means to them. Continue in a similar fashion with the remaining vocabulary words.

ELL Have children make clue cards for all vocabulary words by writing a vocabulary word on the front of each index card and drawing a picture illustrating that word on the back. Stack the cards with the picture sides up. Then have children take turns, showing the picture for each word. Have the other children think of the words. Continue until all children have given an answer.

TARGET SKILL AND STRATEGY

DRAW CONCLUSIONS Remind children that to *draw conclusions* is to think about facts and details from the selection and what they already know and then decide something about the information. Invite students to read page 8. Ask children to draw a conclusion about the importance of learning to cooperate in Korea.

VISUALIZE Remind children that to *visualize* is to form pictures in their minds. As children read page 4, ask: What pictures do you see in your mind? Ask children to be as detailed as possible.

ADDITIONAL SKILL INSTRUCTION

FACT AND OPINION Remind children that a *statement of fact* can be proved true or false. A *statement of opinion* is a statement of a person's belief. Invite children to look for statements of fact and opinion as they read.

Name _____

Draw Conclusions

Draw a line to match each conclusion with the facts and details that support it.

Facts and Details

1. Mina lives in a large city called Seoul.

2. Some things in Seoul are old and some are new.

3. After the morning meeting, the children bow and thank the principal.

4. On New Year's Day, Koreans visit friends and family and share special foods.

Conclusions

a. The children respect their school.

b. New Year's Day is an important holiday in Korea.

c. Mina lives in South Korea.

d. Seoul is an old city.

5. Read the sentences below. Write a sentence to draw a conclusion.

In different parts of the world, children play with balls, sticks, jump ropes, kites, and other toys.

Conclusion:

_____

_____

_____

Name _____

Vocabulary

Read the passage below.
Write the correct vocabulary word in each blank.

Words to Know			
answer	company	faraway	parents
picture	school	wash	

I live in a _____ country in Asia.

I live with my _____ in South Korea.

Last week we had _____. My aunt
visited us from the United States. To prepare for my aunt's visit, I

helped my mother _____ the curtains.

When she arrived, I went to _____

the door. My aunt visited my _____.

I drew a _____ for my aunt to take
home with her. I hope she will remember me.

Arachnid or Insect?

SUMMARY Children discover that all bugs are not insects—some are arachnids. This selection describes the differences among a variety of creepy creatures. Compare and contrast relationships are indicated as the author discusses interesting ways insects and arachnids keep themselves safe.

LESSON VOCABULARY

been	believe
caught	finally
today	tomorrow
whatever	

INTRODUCE THE BOOK

INTRODUCE THE TITLE AND AUTHOR Discuss with children the title and the author of *Arachnid or Insect?* Prompt children to notice the title is a question. Lead them to understand that the title suggests an insect is not the same thing as an arachnid. Ask children how they think this topic relates to science.

BUILD BACKGROUND Encourage children to volunteer what they know about bugs. Have them draw pictures to help them recall the physical features of the creatures that come to mind. Point out different physical features that children included in their drawings.

ELL Many of the English names of bugs may be unfamiliar to children. As the class builds background knowledge, have children share the names of common bugs in their home languages and tell if bugs are considered helpful or harmful. There may be myths, folktales, and songs about bugs in their home cultures that they will want to share.

PREVIEW/TAKE A PICTURE WALK Remind children to keep in mind the title as they preview the book. As children look at the photographs and diagrams, lead them to begin to answer the question posed by the title.

READ THE BOOK

SET PURPOSE Have children talk about which "bugs" they find strange, ugly, pretty, or creepy. Encourage them to think about a particular bug as they read to find out whether that bug is an insect or an arachnid.

STRATEGY SUPPORT: SUMMARIZE Remind children that good readers are able to use their own words to tell the important information in a book. Tell children using their own words to *summarize* shows they understand what they have read. Model this strategy by rereading the page 4 aloud. Say: To tell what happens in my own words, I ask, *what is this page mostly about?* I use my own words to tell, *Insects have 6 legs and 3 body parts.* As children read, have them tell the main idea of each page by asking themselves: What is this page mostly about?

COMPREHENSION QUESTIONS

PAGE 3 What is the reason most people believe that all bugs are insects? *(They have not learned about arachnids.)*

PAGE 5 Which human body parts perform functions similar to an insect's antenna? *(hands and nose)*

PAGE 6 What is the difference between an arachnid's body and an insect's body? *(The arachnid's body has two parts. The insect's body has three parts.)*

PAGE 8 How many legs does a grasshopper have? *(six)*

PAGE 12 Why is it helpful to know the difference between arachnids and insects? *(I will not mix up insects and arachnids anymore.)*

REVISIT THE BOOK

THINK AND SHARE

1. Responses will vary but show understanding of comparing and contrasting insects and arachnids.
2. Possible responses: Insects have six legs, their bodies have three parts, and they can have wings. Arachnids do not have wings, they have eight legs, and their bodies have two parts. Both are sometimes called bugs and have ways to keep safe.
3. *them-selves, grass-hopper, butter-fly, lady-bug, any-more, what-ever*
4. Responses will vary but should include children's reactions to the story.

EXTEND UNDERSTANDING As children get to the first diagram in the book on page 4, prompt them to explain how the labels describe the different physical features of an ant. Ask children if they can understand the meanings of the words *thorax* and *abdomen* by looking at the picture. Ask them to point to the physical features that they share with the ant.

RESPONSE OPTIONS

WRITING Give each child a picture of a bug that is not discussed in the book. Have them write a few sentences about whether the bug in the picture is an insect or arachnid.

SCIENCE CONNECTION

Scientists group living things based on their similarities and differences. Mirror this process of grouping items by asking children to bring in a few objects that they have collected from nature. As a class, put the objects in groups and sub-groups.

Skill Work

TEACH/REVIEW VOCABULARY

Ask children to group the vocabulary words into the categories, *time* and *action*. Have each child write a sentence using one word from each category. Allow time for children to share their sentences with the class. Since the words *whatever* and *been* do not fit in either group, discuss these words and have children use them in sentences to show their meanings.

TARGET SKILL AND STRATEGY

COMPARE AND CONTRAST Explain to children that *compare* and *contrast* is to look for how things are the same and how they are different. During reading, have children compare and contrast arachnids and insects.

SUMMARIZING Remind children they should be able to tell in their own words what the book is about. Tell them that using their own words to explain what the text is mostly about means that they are able to identify the main idea of the text.

ADDITIONAL SKILL INSTRUCTION

MAIN IDEA After reading, prompt children to identify the *main idea* of the book by asking the following questions: What is the book about? *(bugs)* What is the most important idea about this topic? *(Insects are not the same as arachnids.)* Explain that identifying the main idea of the book can help them understand what they read.

Name _____

Compare and Contrast

Answer questions below using what you have learned from *Arachnids or Insects?*

1. List 2 ways arachnids and insects are different.

_____

- -

_____

_____

2. List 2 ways arachnids and insects are the same.

_____

- -

_____

_____

3. Compare two insects from the story. How are they similar?

_____

- -

_____

_____

4. Contrast two arachnids from the story. How are they different?

_____

- -

_____

Name _____

Vocabulary

Draw a line to match each word with its meaning.

Words to Know
been   believe   caught   finally   today   tomorrow   whatever

1. been

a. the next day

2. believe

b. at the end

3. caught

c. anything

4. finally

d. to feel that something is true

5. today

e. this day

6. tomorrow

f. to have stayed or continued

7. whatever

g. grabbed hold of something

8. Write a sentence using the words *believe* and *whatever*.

_____

- - - - - - - - - - - - - - - - - - -

_____

- - - - - - - - - - - - - - - - - - -

_____

- - - - - - - - - - - - - - - - - - -

_____

The International Food Fair!

SUMMARY In this story, a family solves the problem of what to eat for dinner by going to an international food fair. It supports the lesson concept of a creative idea being a solution.

LESSON VOCABULARY

alone	buy
daughters	half
many	their
youngest	

INTRODUCE THE BOOK

INTRODUCE THE TITLE AND AUTHOR Discuss with children the title and the author of *The International Food Fair!* Have children describe what they think is happening in the cover illustration.

BUILD BACKGROUND Ask children to discuss foods they know about that come from other countries. Ask where they tasted that food or who made it for them. Also have them describe any special foods their families may enjoy.

PREVIEW/TAKE A PICTURE WALK Have children look at the pictures in the book before reading. Ask: What do you think this story is about? Have children look at page 12. Ask and discuss: Is this part of the story? What is this part of the book about?

READ THE BOOK

SET PURPOSE Have children set a purpose for reading *The International Food Fair!* Remind children of what they discussed in their preview. Ask: What do you want to learn more about in this story?

STRATEGY SUPPORT: PREDICT AND SET PURPOSE Remind children to look for clues that help them decide what might happen next. Have them think about the main characters and what they might do next. As children read the story, have them make predictions after each page by asking questions. Have them use a three-column predictions chart to list predictions, support predictions, and revisit predictions to see if they are correct or need to be revised.

COMPREHENSION QUESTIONS

PAGES 3–4 Why do you think the parents forgot who was supposed to make dinner? (*Possible response: They are both busy teaching.*)

PAGES 6–7 Why did Amy and Allie wait to get food, and Danny did not? (*Possible response: Since Danny is younger, he is less patient.*)

PAGE 10 What happened in the middle of the story? (*The family ate different kinds of food.*)

PAGE 10 How are a cannoli and a spring roll different? (*A cannoli is a dessert stuffed with cheese and chocolate chips. A spring roll is rolled and fried, made with pork and vegetables.*)

PAGE 11 What did you learn about people by reading this story? (*Possible response: Sharing our differences helps us get along.*)

REVISIT THE BOOK

THINK AND SHARE

1. Possible response: DIm Sum, fufu, crepes, and cannolis.
2. Possible response: I think the Kyles will try international foods again. Some clues are: their children liked to meet students from other countries, they had a good time, and they thought the food was delicious.
3. They introduced the children from oldest to youngest. Danny was born last.
4. Possible response: I would like to try fufu because it sounds tasty.

EXTEND UNDERSTANDING Have children analyze the story's setting. Remind children that a story's setting is where and when the story takes place. Ask: What is the setting at the beginning of the story? What is it at the end?

RESPONSE OPTIONS

WRITING Have children write a description of a favorite food they have eaten at home and how it is made.

SOCIAL STUDIES CONNECTION

Time For SOCIAL STUDIES

Have each child choose one of the countries in the story. Invite children to do guided Internet research to learn about other dishes that are eaten in their countries. Have them share their findings with the class.

Skill Work

TEACH/REVIEW VOCABULARY

Have children make sets of vocabulary word cards. Write the following words on the board: *my, few, together, sell, whole, oldest, sons.* Ask children to show the vocabulary word that is the opposite of each word.

TARGET SKILL AND STRATEGY

SEQUENCE Explain that *sequence* is the order in which story events happen. Remind children that while reading, it is helpful to think of what happens first, next, and last. Ask: What happened first in the story? What happens next? Finally, what happens last?

ELL Give each child a sequence diagram to record what happens in the beginning, middle, and end of the story.

PREDICT AND SET PURPOSE Have children think about what will probably happen next. Tell children to think about the characters and *predict* what they might do next. Remind them to check their predictions to see if they were correct. Encourage them to reread to see why their predictions may have been incorrect. Remind children that thinking about what might happen next will help them understand the big idea of the story.

ADDITIONAL SKILL INSTRUCTION

COMPARE AND CONTRAST Remind children: A *comparison* tells how two or more things are alike and different. A *contrast* tells only how two or more things are different. Clue words, such as *like, as, but,* or *unlike,* can indicate comparisons. Together look on page 4. Ask: How are Mr. and Mrs. Kyle alike? *(Both teach at the college.)* How are they different? *(man/father; woman/mother)* Have children use a Venn diagram to compare and contrast two foods at the fair.

Name _____

Sequence

Sequence refers to the order of events in both fiction and nonfiction. Sequence can also refer to the steps in a process.

Read the events that happened in the story in the box. They are listed out of order. Put them in order by writing the letter of the step on the correct line below.

---

a. The Kyle family went to the International Food Fair.

b. All of the children tried a cannoli.

c. Mr. and Mrs. Kyle did not know whose turn it was to cook dinner.

d. The children learned about fufu.

e. The family learned what the word Dim sum meant.

---

1. _____

2. _____

3. _____

4. _____

5. _____

Name _____

Vocabulary

Draw a line from each word to the word that means the opposite.

Words to Know

alone	buy	daughters	half
many	their	youngest	

1. alone   a. few

2. buy   b. oldest

3. daughters   c. our

4. half   d. together

5. many   e. sell

6. their   f. whole

7. youngest   g. sons

Thomas Adams: Chewing Gum Inventor

SUMMARY This is a biography of the inventor of modern chewing gum, Thomas Adams. By describing how his idea for a new gum came through a chance meeting, the book shows where new ideas can come from.

LESSON VOCABULARY

clothes	hours
money	neighbor
only	question
taught	

INTRODUCE THE BOOK

INTRODUCE THE TITLE AND AUTHOR Discuss with children the title and the author of *Thomas Adams: Chewing Gum Inventor*. Tell them that this is a biography, a story of a person's life. Ask children to discuss other biographies they may have read.

BUILD BACKGROUND Ask children to share what they know about chewing gum. Ask: What do you think chewing gum is made from? How long do you think it has been around?

PREVIEW/TAKE A PICTURE WALK Have children look at the pictures and captions in the book before reading. Ask: Who do you think this book is about? What makes him special? What kinds of projects did he work on? What can you figure out from the illustration on page 6?

READ THE BOOK

SET PURPOSE Have children set a purpose for reading *Thomas Adams: Chewing Gum Inventor*. Ask: What would you like to know about Thomas Adams?

STRATEGY SUPPORT: INFERRING Help children understand that when they *infer* they use facts and details in the text, along with what they already know, to learn something new. Inferring will help children make a decision or opinion about what they have read. Model inferring on page 5. Say: I read that Santa Ana taught Adams about a rubbery substance called chicle. I know that tires are made from rubber. I can infer that Adams is going to make a new tire out of chicle. Ask children to think about details of the story as they read.

ELL Support comprehension by reviewing comparative and superlative adjectives: *best* (page 4), *cheaper* (page 5), and *happier* (page 8). Show children how these words are formed.

COMPREHENSION QUESTIONS

PAGE 3 Why do you think chewing gum has been around for so long? *(Possible answer: People have always liked to chew and taste, even when they are not eating.)*

PAGE 8 Why did the storeowner agree to sell a new gum? *(Possible response: If it sold better, he would make more money.)*

PAGE 11 Why did Adams make a lot of money? *(He sold a lot of gum.)*

PAGE 12 Do you think Adams was a great inventor? *(Possible response: Yes, he turned a fun idea into a great product.)*

REVISIT THE BOOK

THINK AND SHARE

1. Responses will vary but should include facts and opinions with corresponding page numbers.
2. Responses will vary but should show use of combining prior knowledge with the text to make them continue to read.
3. Since his neighbor was also there, and a neighbor is someone who lives near you, they were probably both near their homes.
4. Possible response: Dentyne gum appeared in 1899.

EXTEND UNDERSTANDING Point out the time line on page 12. Ask: How does the time line help us understand the world of chewing gum? Guide children to see how it shows events in the development of chewing gum in chronological order.

RESPONSE OPTIONS

WRITING Have children write three to four sentences that summarize the importance of Thomas Adams or other inventors.

SOCIAL STUDIES CONNECTION

Provide biographies of other American inventors. Have each child choose one book to read. Invite children to give oral presentations on what they have read.

Skill Work

TEACH/REVIEW VOCABULARY

Write the vocabulary words and these word groups on the board: *alone, once; problem, puzzle; costume, outfit; cash, coins; time, period; friend, next-door; schooled, trained.* Have children say the vocabulary word that best belongs with each group as you read the group aloud.

TARGET SKILL AND STRATEGY

FACT AND OPINION Explain to children that a statement of *fact* can be proved true or false and a statement of *opinion* expresses a belief or feeling. Ask children to locate one fact and one opinion in *Thomas Adams: Chewing Gum Inventor*. For example, the sentence on page 5, Adams met a man named Antonio Lopez de Santa Anna, is a fact. The sentence on page 9, chewing gum was much better than wax gum, is an opinion.

INFERRING Remind children that using facts and details from the text, along with what they know, will help them learn something new. After reading the story, tell children to infer by reviewing the details and facts. Ask: Could Thomas Adams have thought of inventing chewing gum without seeing the girl in the drugstore? What details lead you to this conclusion?

ADDITIONAL SKILL INSTRUCTION

DRAW CONCLUSIONS Tell children that they should use what they have read and what they know about real life to *draw conclusions*, or figure out more about what happens in the book. After page 8, ask: Why do you think the storeowner wanted to sell the new gum? *(The book says gum was popular and I know that storeowners want to sell a lot and make more money, so the owner probably thought the gum would help make money for him.)*

Name _____

Fact and Opinion

Read the sentences below. They each are a **fact** or an **opinion** from *Thomas Adams: Chewing Gum Inventor*. Then write them in the correct column.

Thomas Adams was born in 1818.

Adams was a well-dressed man.

He had sons.

Adams best invention was chewing gum.

Chicle is used in chewing gum and comes from Mexico.

Chewing gum is better than wax gum.

Fact

1. _____

2. _____

3. _____

Opinion

4. _____

5. _____

6. _____

Name _____

Vocabulary

Draw a line to match each word with its clue.

Words to Know
clothes hours money neighbor
only question taught

1. clothes

2. hours

3. money

4. neighbor

5. only

6. question

7. taught

a. could be coins

b. just this one

c. what the teacher did

d. something to ask

e. parts of a day

f. something to wear

g. lives on your street

8. Write a sentence using two words from the box.

_____

_____

_____

_____

_____

Making Traveling Fun

SUMMARY Children read ways that they can keep themselves entertained on a long car trip.

LESSON VOCABULARY

clearing	crashed
perfect	pond
splashing	spilling
traveled	

INTRODUCE THE BOOK

INTRODUCE THE TITLE AND AUTHOR Discuss the title and author of *Making Traveling Fun*. Based on the title and the illustration on the cover, ask children to describe what they think this book might be about. Ask children what the characters are holding and why they might have chosen those particular toys.

BUILD BACKGROUND Discuss car trips with children. Have them tell where they have traveled to, with whom, and how they passed the time. For those children who have never taken an extended car trip, explain that it is sometimes easy to get bored and that it helps to bring along things to make the time go by more quickly.

PREVIEW/TAKE A PICTURE WALK Invite children to take a picture walk to preview the text and illustrations. Discuss what the characters are doing and whether children did those same activities on the car trips they've taken.

READ THE BOOK

SET PURPOSE Have children set a purpose for reading *Making Traveling Fun*. Suggest that one purpose for reading this story could be to find ways to have more fun on their next car trip.

STRATEGY SUPPORT: BACKGROUND KNOWLEDGE Tell children that when we read, we often make connections to something we already know about. Point out that good readers are always using their background knowledge to help them make sense of what they're reading, or to help them adjust their thinking as they read. Encourage children to think of their own experiences as they read.

COMPREHENSION QUESTIONS

PAGE 3 Why do you think the author asked this question at the very beginning of the book? *(She wanted me to start thinking about car trips I've taken so I would understand the point of the story.)*

PAGES 4–6 Based on your experiences with car trips, what other suggestions might you have that would fall into the categories on these pages—using your imagination, drinks, and snacks? *(Possible responses: Don't drink too much or you'll have to stop to use the bathroom more frequently; bring snacks that don't need to be refrigerated, or else you'll have to bring a cooler.)*

PAGES 7–9 What do you think about the toys, games, and other things to do that are in this story? *(Possible responses: It seems silly to bring balls, since you can't throw them in the car; maps are good to look at to figure out where you are, games are always good.)* Are there other ideas you have about how to pass the time on a car trip? *(Possible responses: Some cars have video players so you can watch movies; you can use earphones to listen to music; you can read a book.)*

REVISIT THE BOOK

THINK AND SHARE

1. If you plan ahead, you can do lots of things to make the time pass quickly.
2. Possible response: I already knew that it was easy to get bored on a long car trip.
3. (page 3) Possible response: What *perfect* means: I think it means that nothing goes wrong or that nothing is wrong with something. Something I think is perfect: a sunny day, about 73 degrees.
4. Responses will vary but should include details from the story.

EXTEND UNDERSTANDING Explain to children that taking a long car trip can be fun and cost less than taking an airplane trip. If you take a car trip, you don't have to arrive at an airport way ahead of your flight, and you can get out of the car to stretch your legs whenever you want to. And when you get where you're going, you already have a car to get around with and don't have to rent one.

RESPONSE OPTIONS

LANGUAGE ARTS Have children work in small groups to make up a game that can be played on a long car trip. They should include rules and any objects or props that are needed to play the game. Then ask each group to tell the rest of the class about their games.

SOCIAL STUDIES CONNECTION

Provide children with a copy of a map that goes from one major city near you to another. Have them figure out the route to take on the map and use the map key to figure out how long the trip will take. Provide assistance as needed.

ELL To help children understand why people take long car trips, provide a web for children. In the center of the web, write: taking a car trip. Then ask children to think of reasons they might take a long car trip and help them write the reasons in the outer circles on the web.

Skill Work

TEACH/REVIEW VOCABULARY

Write each vocabulary word on a small piece of paper. Fold up the papers and place them in a basket or other container. Have children take turns reaching into the basket and taking a piece of paper. Children have to define the word they picked and use it in a sentence. When their turn is done, have children put the paper back into the basket to be picked by someone else.

TARGET SKILL AND STRATEGY

DRAW CONCLUSIONS Remind children that when they *draw conclusions*, they are making a decision about something, based on facts, details, and what they already know. Have children look at the cover illustration again. Ask: What conclusion can you draw about why the children might have a basketball and a football with them? Lead them to conclude that since you need a large space in order to play ball, they must be traveling to a place that has a field or basketball court.

BACKGROUND KNOWLEDGE Remind children that *background knowledge* is the information about a subject that they already know. Ask children to discuss how thinking about what they already knew about car trips helped them understand what they read.

ADDITIONAL SKILL INSTRUCTION

MAIN IDEA Remind children that the *main idea* of a book is the "big idea." Then remind them that the main idea is different than the topic of a book, and that the main idea is often stated in one of the beginning paragraphs in a text. Ask: What is the main idea in *Making Traveling Fun*?

Name_____

Draw Conclusions

Complete the chart below by writing four facts about the characters and drawing a conclusion from those facts.

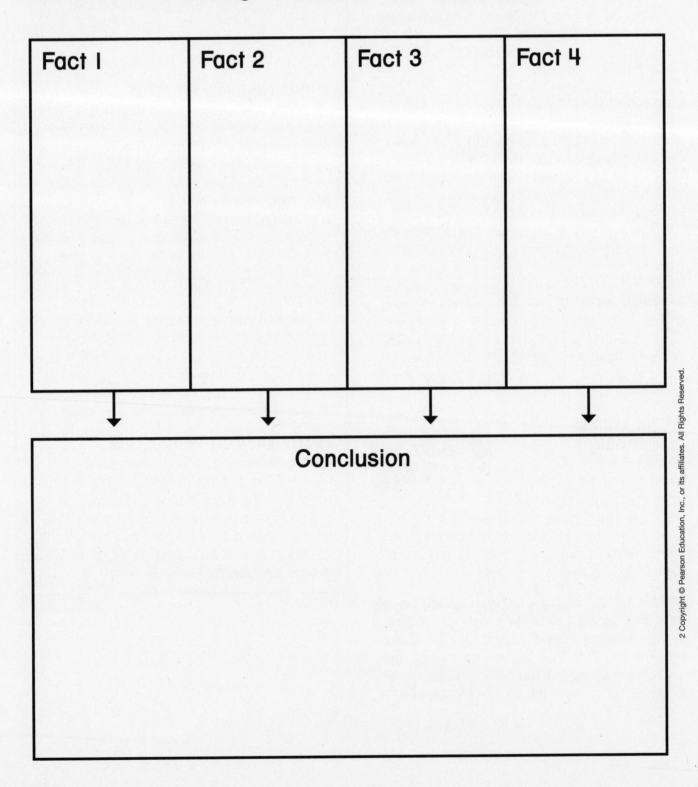

Fact 1	Fact 2	Fact 3	Fact 4

Conclusion

Name_____

Vocabulary

Complete the chart below by putting a check mark in the column that tells what kind of word each is.

Vocabulary Word	Person, Place or Thing	Action Word	Describing Word
clearing			
crashed			
perfect			
pond			
splashing			
spilling			
traveled			

How Do Plants Grow?

SUMMARY This informational text describes different types of plants and the essential things that all plants need to change and grow.

LESSON VOCABULARY

bumpy	fruit
harvest	roots
smooth	soil
vines	

INTRODUCE THE BOOK

INTRODUCE THE TITLE AND AUTHOR Discuss with children the title and the author of *How Do Plants Grow?* Based on the title and cover photograph, ask the children what they think they might learn from this book. Also call attention to the Science label in the upper-left corner and ask children how they think the information in this book might be related to science.

BUILD BACKGROUND Invite the children to talk about the different plants they have seen using as descriptive language as possible (size, color, shape of leaves, scent). Children who have a garden or potted plants at home may wish to share what they know about caring for plants.

PREVIEW/TAKE A PICTURE WALK Have the children preview the book, looking at the pictures. Ask them to discuss the photographs, naming the flowers and plants they know and asking questions about those they don't. Also encourage children to describe the attributes of the plants that are pictured, such as tall trees, prickly cactus, bumpy bark, smooth petals.

READ THE BOOK

SET PURPOSE Based on your background discussion and preview of the book, invite the children to share what they would like to learn about from this text. Ask: What do you think will be most interesting about this book? Are there any photographs in this book that you want to know more about?

STRATEGY SUPPORT: IMPORTANT IDEAS Explain to children that *important ideas* are the supporting details or facts for the main idea in the story. Knowing the important ideas can help children understand the author's purpose for writing a story. These details can be the sequence of the story, special fonts, or illustrations. Tell children to look for important ideas as they read.

COMPREHENSION QUESTIONS

PAGE 5 (ALSO 6, 8, 10) What are the three things that plants need to live and grow? *(Water, light, and air.)*

PAGES 8-9 Look at the photographs on pages 8 and 9. What has happened to each of these flowers and why? *(Healthy daisy has gotten a lot of light; dead daisy got very little light.)*

PAGE 11 Describe how plants and animals share the air and why plants and animals need each other. *(Animals breathe in oxygen and breathe out carbon dioxide; plants take in carbon dioxide and give off oxygen.)*

PAGE 12 Read the first sentence on page 12. Is this a fact? How can you tell? *(Fact: it can be proved true or false.)*

REVISIT THE BOOK
READER RESPONSE

1. Possible responses: All plants are different, but they are alike in some ways; Air is made up of many different gases; When plants get what they need, they grow healthy and strong.

2. Responses will vary but answer should include details of how plants grow and how it helped as they read.

3. Page 12: apple

4. Possible response: It helped me to remember that a tree is a plant, and it helped me see how tall some trees can grow.

EXTEND UNDERSTANDING Invite the children to look again at the photographs in the book. Call attention to the captions and labels and discuss how these can aid in comprehension. Ask: Why do you think the author included the captions and labels with the photographs? How do these features help us better understand the information in the book?

RESPONSE OPTIONS

WRITING To extend learning have the children make a KWL chart that includes something they now know from reading the text and something they would like to learn more about. Provide children with additional books about plants and have them complete their charts with new information they have learned.

SCIENCE CONNECTION

As a class project, plant flowers or vegetables in small containers. Keep them on a windowsill or in a greenhouse where the children can take turns caring for the plants and monitoring their growth.

Skill Work

TEACH/REVIEW VOCABULARY

Guide the children in writing a few related sentences using each of the vocabulary words.

ELL To help children better understand the definitions of the adjectives, go on a "sensory hunt" to find things that are bumpy and smooth. Describe what you feel, saying, for example, "The top of the desk is smooth. This gravel is bumpy."

TARGET SKILL AND STRATEGY

SEQUENCE Tell children the *sequence* is the order in which story events happen. Explain that bold words and illustrations in the story can help them figure out when each event occurs. Have children turn to page 6. Ask: What happens first? After the nutrients is absorbed what happens next? Finally, what happens last?

IMPORTANT IDEAS Remind children that *important ideas* are facts and details that support the main idea. These ideas can help them understand the author's purpose for writing the story. Model finding important ideas. Say: I know this story is about how plants grow. I read that all plants need sunlight to grow.

ADDITIONAL SKILL INSTRUCTION

CAUSE AND EFFECT Model for children how to understand cause and effect by identifying what has happened and why. Draw attention to the information on page 7. Ask: How have desert plants learned to adapt? (*Store water in stems; live for a long time on little water.*) Why have they had to adapt? (*Because deserts don't get much rain.*)

Name _____

Sequence

Read the events that happened in the story in the box. They are listed out of order. Put them in order by writing the letter of the step on the correct line below.

a. Animals breath out carbon dioxide and plants take in carbon dioxide.

b. The leaves use nutrients in water to make food.

c. Plants use the sunlight that falls on their leaves to make food.

d. Some large plants start as tiny seeds and grow into large plants.

e. We know plants are at work when they produce fruit.

I. _____ _____

2. _____ _____

3. _____ _____

4. _____ _____

5. _____ _____

Name _____

Vocabulary

Draw a line to match the word to the picture.

1. fruit

2. roots

3. soil

4. vines

5. harvest

a.

b.

c.

d.

e.

List two things that are bumpy and three things that are smooth.

bumpy

smooth

A Slice of Mud Pie

SUMMARY In this fiction story, Mr. Fernando teaches his class about soil. His students learn what makes up soil. They also learn how worms help the soil.

LESSON VOCABULARY

grains	materials
particles	seep
substances	texture

INTRODUCE THE BOOK

INTRODUCE THE TITLE AND AUTHOR Discuss with children the title and author of *A Slice of Mud Pie*. After looking at the cover and title, have children tell you what they think will happen in the story.

BUILD BACKGROUND Discuss what children know about soil. Explain that we often call soil *dirt*, but that dirt is just the top layer of soil. Ask: Have you ever played in soil or taken care of plants? Have you ever made mud pies? Have children tell you what they've seen in soil and what soil feels like.

PREVIEW/TAKE A PICTURE WALK Invite children to look at the pictures in *A Slice of Mud Pie*. Ask them what they think the setting of the story is, and why they think so.

READ THE BOOK

SET PURPOSE Have children set a purpose for reading *A Slice of Mud Pie*. Say: Look at the picture on the cover again. What do you think you will find out about soil? What do you most want to learn about soil?

STRATEGY SUPPORT: QUESTIONING Remind children that there are several ways to find answer to questions. Some answers might be "right there" in the book. For other answers, children may need to use both what is in the book and what they already know. Tell children that this is a strategy that will help them as they are asked questions about a story.

COMPREHENSION QUESTIONS

PAGE 3 Where does this story take place? (*Mr. Fernando's classroom*)

PAGE 6 Look at the picture of soil Mr. Fernando is standing near. What are three parts of soil? (*dirt, sand, rock*)

PAGE 7 How do worms help soil? (*Worms make sure the soil has air.*)

PAGE 9 What is full of substances that help plants grow? (*rain*)

REVISIT THE BOOK

THINK AND SHARE

1. Responses will vary but children should list one opinion from the story and one about the story.
2. Possible response: What is in soil? The story taught me there was air, water, and sand in soil.
3. sounds, out, four, our, your, ground, growled, own, down, brown, frown, now, know, below, grow; sentences will vary.
4. Responses will vary but should relate to the story.

EXTEND UNDERSTANDING Explain to children that this is a fiction story in which facts are taught. Ask them to identify which parts of the story are fiction and which parts are fact. Guide them to be able to tell the difference.

RESPONSE OPTIONS

WRITING Have children imagine how a worm would view the world. Invite them to write a paragraph describing what a worm would see as it crawls down through some soil.

SCIENCE CONNECTION

Encourage children to find more information about soil. They can use the library, books in the classroom, or do research on the Internet.

Skill Work

TEACH/REVIEW VOCABULARY

Give children vocabulary cards. Have students look for the words in the story. When they find a word, they can copy that sentence on the vocabulary card.

ELL Pair more-proficient English speakers with less-proficient ones for the vocabulary activity above.

TARGET SKILL AND STRATEGY

FACT AND OPINION After reading, remind children that a statement of opinion is someone's judgment, belief, or feelings and that a statement of fact can be proved true or false. Help children locate one fact and one opinion in the text. For example on page 5, *That sounds great!* is an opinion and *We'll be looking at mud pies today.* is a fact. Allow time for children to share with the class.

QUESTIONING Remind children that questions should be answered completely and correctly. There are several ways to find an answer to a question. The answer might be "right there" in the text, you may need to use what you already know, or you may use both to answer in the text *and* what you know to give a complete and correct answer. Ask: What is in humus? (The answer is on page 10.)

ADDITIONAL SKILL INSTRUCTION

SETTING Help children define the meaning of setting. Discuss the setting of *A Slice of Soil*. After reading page 3, have children tell which sentence identifies the setting.

Name _____

Fact and Opinion

> Soil is made up of sand grains, air, water, and humus. Sand grains are small particles of rock. Air spaces let rain seep into the soil. The plants suck up the water. Humus is little pieces of dead animals and plants.

Write two facts from the paragraph.

_____
- -
_____
- -
_____
- -
_____

Write a statement of opinion on why soil is important.

_____
- -
_____
- -
_____
- -
_____

Name _____

Vocabulary

WORD SEARCH

Find and circle the following words. All words go from left to right.

Words to Know		
grains	materials	particles
seep	substances	texture

```
K E W E I L S U B S T A N C E S
M R Q O A Z X L K F G Y N B H T
T E X T U R E P E W Q C A S D I
T Y B D K G R A I N S P I W C S
M N X A E M Q Y I L A F N C T U
Q S X R T U O P L K M A X M P L
H G F L I W E U Y T V C A Q S J
K O Y S D P A R T I C L E S O O
H G D S T O U W C H I X Z W P I
M A X F J B N S J A V M P J L K
J F E I T L W O P M S E E P A F
Q W S K L J G H A Z D L I W L O
C B X A Z M Q T Y I O D S G H J
L S M A T E R I A L S W Q O G O
```

Too Many Frogs!

SUMMARY Children read about a boy who has a few too many pets.

LESSON VOCABULARY

balance	canyons	coral
rattle	slivers	sway
whisper		

INTRODUCE THE BOOK

INTRODUCE THE TITLE AND AUTHOR Discuss the title and author of *Too Many Frogs!* Based on the title and the illustration on the cover, ask children to describe what they think this book might be about. Ask children how many frogs they can count in the picture.

BUILD BACKGROUND Discuss having a pet with children. Have children think about what kinds of animals make good pets and the responsibilities of keeping a pet.

PREVIEW/TAKE A PICTURE WALK Invite children to take a picture walk to preview the text and illustrations. Discuss how Josh finds his pet.

READ THE BOOK

SET PURPOSE Have children set a purpose for reading *Too Many Frogs!* Ask them to think about how having a pet can affect a family's life.

STRATEGY SUPPORT: VISUALIZE Tell children that good readers form a picture in their minds as they read. Explain that they should *visualize* as they read to make sure they understand what they are reading. Model questions to ask while reading: What would it be like to be in this scene? What would it feel like? Do I understand what is being described?

COMPREHENSION QUESTIONS

PAGES 3–4 What is Josh's problem at the beginning of the story? *(He feels lonely in his room.)*

PAGE 7 What happens after Josh brings Hoppy the frog home? *(He decides he needs more frogs.)*

PAGE 8 Why is Josh's mom upset? *(She thinks there are too many pets in the house. They are making a mess. Hoppy 6 jumped on her head when she walked into Josh's room.)*

PAGE 10 Which sentence tells the main thing that Josh learns in this story? *(A pet was fun, but maybe eight frogs were just too many!)*

REVISIT THE BOOK

THINK AND SHARE

1. Possible response: Josh feels lonely and wants a pet. After he finds his pet frog, Hoppy, he decides to get more frogs. Soon, there are too many frogs in the house. Josh decides to keep Hoppy but take the other frogs back to the pond.

2. Possible response: eeek, jumped, wet, spilled, balance, croaked, mess

3. Possible response: wind, bushes, blew

4. Answers will vary but make sure that children understand the concept of owning pets and the responsibility of caring for them.

EXTEND UNDERSTANDING Explain to children that some animals can be very good pets, but others are not. Discuss what it takes for an animal to be a good pet. For example, pets should be easy to feed and enjoy being around people. They should not be too messy to clean up after.

ELL List a few types of pets on the board, such as *dogs*, *cats*, *lizards*, *fish*, and *birds*. Then have children brainstorm what they know about each type of pet and how to care for them. Write their ideas on the board.

RESPONSE OPTIONS

ART Have children brainstorm some of their favorite animals and whether they would make good pets or not. Have children draw a picture of their favorite animal and write brief statement about whether or not it would make a good pet.

SCIENCE CONNECTION

Provide a large variety of books about frogs and other invertebrates for children to look through. Have children choose one animal to learn more about. Ask children to write a brief report on their animal. Have them illustrate their report with a drawing of the animal.

Skill Work

TEACH/REVIEW VOCABULARY

Have children find the word *rattle* on page 5. Ask a volunteer to explain its meaning. Ask what surrounding words or sentences gave clues to the meaning. Repeat for each vocabulary word.

TARGET SKILL AND STRATEGY

PLOT AND THEME Remind children that the *plot* is the sequence of events that happen in a story, or the problem that gets resolved during the story. The *theme* is the important idea or lesson that can be learned from the story. Give children a few events from the story out of order and have them place the events in correct sequence. Discuss with children the important lesson they can take from the story.

VISUALIZE Remind children that *visualizing* is forming a picture in their minds as they read. Ask children to describe the picture they have in their minds of what Josh's bedroom was like with all those frogs.

ADDITIONAL SKILL INSTRUCTION

REALISM AND FANTASY Remind children that a *realistic* story tells about something that could happen, and a *fantasy* is a story about something that could not happen. Direct children's attention to the illustrations and text on pages 9 and 10 and ask children whether the things the frogs are doing in the house are realistic or a fantasy.

Name_____

Plot and Theme

Complete the chart to show what happens in the beginning, middle, and end of *Too Many Frogs!*

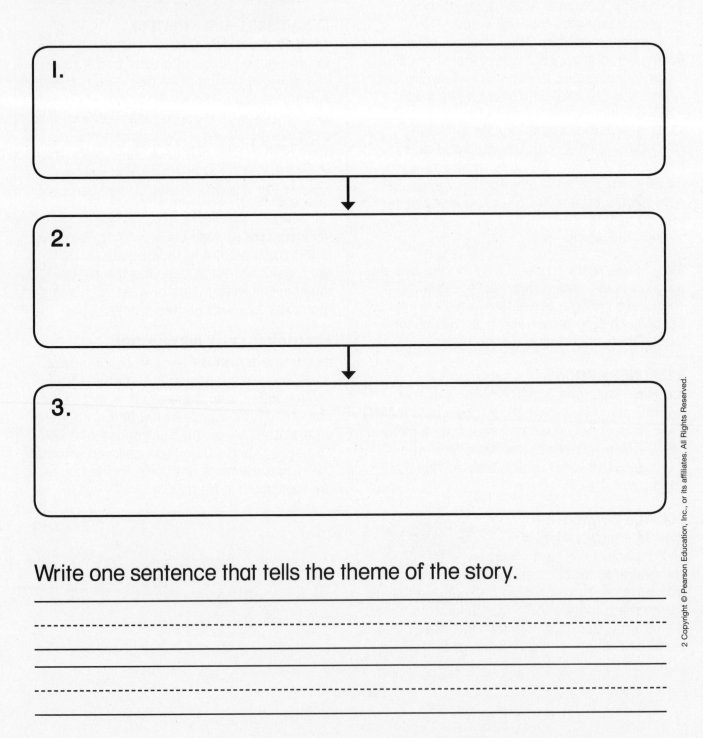

Write one sentence that tells the theme of the story.

_____

- -

_____

- -

_____

Vocabulary

Draw a line from each word to its meaning.

| Words to Know |
| balance   canyons   coral |
| rattle   slivers away   whisper |

1. balance

a. small, thin piece

2. canyons

b. move side to side

3. coral

c. a soft sound

4. rattle

d. hard substance found in the sea

5. slivers

e. the sound a rattlesnake makes

6. sway

f. even on both sides

7. whisper

g. a deep valley

8. Write a sentence using at least one word from the box.

_____

- -

_____

- -

_____

Rainbow Crow Brings Fire to Earth

SUMMARY Children read a Native American myth about how fire came to the world.

LESSON VOCABULARY

awaken   cliffs   mountain

prize   rainbow   suffer

volcano

INTRODUCE THE BOOK

INTRODUCE THE TITLE AND AUTHOR Discuss the title and author of *Rainbow Crow Brings Fire to Earth*. Based on the title and the illustration on the cover, ask children to describe what they think this book might be about. Ask children to describe the bird pictured in the cover illustration.

BUILD BACKGROUND Discuss the many uses of fire with children. Have children think about what fire does and why it has been important to people over the years.

PREVIEW/TAKE A PICTURE WALK Invite children to take a picture walk to preview the text and illustrations. Discuss what happens as the snow and cold come down on the animals.

READ THE BOOK

SET PURPOSE Have children set a purpose for reading *Rainbow Crow Brings Fire to Earth*. Ask them to think about how a bird might bring fire to the earth.

STRATEGY SUPPORT: MONITOR AND CLARIFY Tell children that good readers know that what they read must make sense. Explain that they should check as they read to make sure they understand what they are reading. Model questions to ask while reading: What does this mean? Does this make sense? Do I understand this?

COMPREHENSION QUESTIONS

PAGES 5–6 What happens that makes a problem for the animals? (*It begins to snow.*)

PAGES 7–8 What does Rainbow Crow plan to do to help his friends? (*fly up to the Great Sky Spirit and get the snow to stop*)

PAGE 11 How does Great Spirit give fire to Rainbow Crow? (*He lights the end of a stick with fire and gives it to Rainbow Crow.*

PAGE 13 What is the important thing that Crow gains because of helping his friends? (*He gains his freedom.*)

REVISIT THE BOOK

THINK AND SHARE

1. Plot: Rainbow Crow tries to stop the winter snow to help his friends. The Great Sky Spirit cannot stop the snow and cold, but gives Rainbow Crow fire to help keep the animals warm. Rainbow Crow helps his friends, but loses his beauty and fine voice. The Great Sky Spirit rewards Rainbow Crow for his good deed by giving him freedom. Theme: Rainbow Crow sacrifices his beauty and fine voice to save his friends, but is rewarded with freedom.

2. Responses will vary, but make sure children identify features of the story that were difficult to understand, and how they clarified their questions.

3. Possible responses: a volcano has a hot center that sometimes overflows, and a mountain does not.

4. Responses will vary but should include an experience about sacrifice.

EXTEND UNDERSTANDING Explain to children that many cultures have created stories like myths to tell the story of their people or explain things about the natural world. Discuss how Rainbow Crow's journey gives an explanation for how fire came into the world, and its importance.

RESPONSE OPTIONS

ART Have children imagine an animal or bird without its distinct characteristics, such as a zebra without its stripes or a giraffe with a short neck. Have children draw a picture of their animal, name their new animal, and write a few sentences about how it wins back its distinctive feature.

DRAMA CONNECTION

Work with children to create a readers theater version of the *Rainbow Crow Brings Fire to Earth*. Have children work in small groups to write dialogue for each character in the myth. Have groups take turns presenting the story of Rainbow Crow with the animals and the Great Sky Spirit.

Skill Work

TEACH/REVIEW VOCABULARY

Remind children that when they come to an unfamiliar word, they should look at its sentence and surrounding sentences for clues to its meaning. Direct children to find the word *suffer* on page 8. Ask a volunteer to explain its meaning. Ask what surrounding words or sentences gave clues to the meaning. Repeat for each vocabulary word.

ELL Use pictures to reinforce the meanings of *mountain*, *volcano*, and *rainbow*.

TARGET SKILL AND STRATEGY

PLOT AND THEME Remind children that the *plot* is the sequence of events that happen in a story, or the problem that gets resolved during the story. The *theme* is the important idea or lesson that can be learned from the story. Give children a few events from the story out of order and have them place the events in correct sequence. Discuss with children the important lesson they can take away from the story.

MONITOR AND CLARIFY As they read, encourage children to identify places in the story that confuse them. Have them write down these page numbers so they may return to them after finishing the story. Ask them if these questions have been clarified.

ADDITIONAL SKILL INSTRUCTION

MAIN IDEA Remind children that the *main idea* is the most important idea from a story. Sometimes a main idea is expressed in one sentence in the story, and sometimes the reader has to decide what it is. Encourage children to find the main idea of *Rainbow Crow Brings Fire to Earth*.

Name_____

Plot and Theme

Choose the sentences that tell the problem and solution from the story. Write them in the correct box.

Rainbow Crow loses his bright colors and his voice.

The animals know that someone must travel to the sky.

The snow and cold is making the animals suffer.

Rainbow Crow brings back fire from the Great Spirit.

Problem

↓

Solution

Write one sentence that tells the theme of the story.

_____

_____
_____

_____

Name_____

Vocabulary

Choose the word from the box that best completes each sentence.
Use each word only once.

Words to Know			
awaken	cliffs	mountain	prize
rainbow	suffer	volcano	

1. The park ranger lives on top of a _____ .

2. The thunder might _____ my little sister.

3. We will really _____ if it gets much colder.

4. The _____ came out right after the rainstorm.

5. A _____ is given to the winner.

6. Our teacher took us on a field trip to view the
_____
_____ .

7. The _____ began to rumble and shake.

Keeping Our Community Safe

SUMMARY When things go wrong in a community, a team of emergency workers work together to help people. From the 911 operator to the firefighting team to the EMTs and police officers, and ultimately doctors and nurses, many people work together in a community when people need help.

LESSON VOCABULARY

buildings	burning	masks
quickly	roar	station
tightly		

INTRODUCE THE BOOK

INTRODUCE THE TITLE AND AUTHOR Have children look at the title. Based on the title, ask children what kind of information they think this book will provide. Have children study the cover and answer the question with the community worker they see. Ask children how they know this person is a firefighter, and talk about the clues that helped them form this idea.

BUILD BACKGROUND Suggest to children that a small fire broke out. Ask children which community workers would come to help. Confirm that firefighters and police officers would probably arrive, as well as people in ambulances in case someone was hurt. Explain that these workers help us during emergencies. Speculate with children other people who might work during an emergency, and write down children's ideas.

PREVIEW/TAKE A PICTURE WALK Have children leaf through the book, and encourage them to look for the emergency workers mentioned in the above discussion—firefighters, police officers, EMTs. Ask children to identify other emergency workers they see. For example, which emergency worker do they see on page 4? Which helpers do they see on pages 8 and 9?

READ THE BOOK

SET PURPOSE Encourage children to set a purpose for reading this book. Ask children to express what intrigues them about the book cover and title. Have children form their ideas as questions. Tell children to think about their questions as they read and to look for the answers to their questions in the text.

STRATEGY SUPPORT: IMPORTANT IDEAS Explain to children that *important ideas* or supporting details can be presented as headings, illustrations, key words, and the sequence of the text. Ask students to browse the book before reading to find possible important ideas then make note of them while reading.

COMPREHENSION QUESTIONS

PAGE 5 What is the main idea of this page? *(This page describes what EMTs do.)*

PAGES 8-9 How do doctors help during an emergency? *(They take care of people who are sick or injured during an emergency.)*

PAGE 15 What is the sequence of events on this page? *(EMTs call the nurses. Nurses and doctors wait for the ambulance. They rush people to the emergency room once they arrive.)*

PAGE 15 What might happen if a community worker did not do his or her job? *(People might not be saved. The emergency could get worse.)*

REVISIT THE BOOK

READER RESPONSE

1. An opinion because it is a belief.
2. They told me what kind of worker I would learn about in each section. The information was organized according to types of community workers.
3. Sentences will vary, but should use *quickly* and *tightly* as adverbs.
4. Answers will vary but should include prior knowledge and show understanding of the text.

EXTEND UNDERSTANDING Point out to children that this book explores how community workers work as a team during a fire. Elicit from children other emergencies that community workers might respond to, such as a car accident, a burglary, a weather emergency, someone getting very ill, and so on. Talk about the community workers that would respond in each scenario. Help children conclude that emergency workers help us not only during fires, but any time that people need help.

RESPONSE OPTIONS

WRITING Have children write an ad, looking for people to be community helpers. Tell children to write why the jobs are important and why community helpers are needed.

LISTENING AND SPEAKING Being able to talk to an emergency operator is an important skill. Have children role-play calling 911 to report a fire at the school. Ask questions that an emergency operator might ask, such as the location of the fire, if anyone is hurt, where the child is calling from, and so on. Tell children to listen closely to your questions and to answer as best they can. Remind children that in order for the emergency worker to understand the caller, the caller needs to speak clearly.

SOCIAL STUDIES CONNECTION

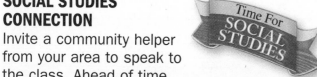

Invite a community helper from your area to speak to the class. Ahead of time, have children create a list of questions to ask the community helper. Encourage children to ask their questions at the appropriate time.

Skill Work

TEACH/REVIEW VOCABULARY

Have children look through the book and apply the vocabulary words to the pictures. For example, the 911 operator works at a telephone *station*. The operator works *quickly* to alert others about the emergency.

ELL Invite children to role-play being firefighters as they use the vocabulary. For example, children can pretend to slip on masks, work *quickly*, leave the *station,* and approach a *burning building,* holding onto their hoses *tightly.*

TARGET SKILL AND STRATEGY

FACT AND OPINION Practice locating a statement of fact and a statement of opinion with children. Remind children that a statement of *opinion* is a feeling or belief and a statement of *fact* can be proved. Invite the children to look through the book locating facts. Then ask the children to write down 2 statements of opinion based on the book.

IMPORTANT IDEAS After reading, review with children that *important ideas* are the supporting details in the story that can be presented in various forms. Ask: How did the headings help you better understand the main idea? How did the pictures help? Did the sequence of the story help you understand the main idea?

ADDITIONAL SKILL INSTRUCTION

CAUSE AND EFFECT Share with children that the action that makes something happen is the *cause.* The result of that action is the *effect.* On the board, draw a box labeled *Cause* and write *A fire starts.* Draw an arrow connecting the Cause box to an Effect box. Ask: What might happen if a fire starts? List children's ideas on the board in the *Effects* box.

Name _____

Fact and Opinion

Read the passage below. Draw a line from each sentence on the left to the words fact or opinion.

> There are many different community workers. 911 operators quickly send out help in an emergency. EMT workers drive people to the hospital so a doctor can see them. Firefighters save peoples' houses by putting out fires. Police officers make sure everyone follows the rules and stays safe.

1. There are many different community workers.

2. An EMT is better than a doctor.

3. Firefighters are brave because they put out fires.

4. Police help keep the community safe.

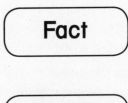

Fact

Opinion

5. Write a sentence that is a fact about community workers.

_____

_____

_____

Name _____

Vocabulary

The paragraph below tells about an emergency, but some words are missing. **Read** the paragraph and fill in the correct missing words from the box.

Hint: The part of speech has been given to help you.

Words to Know

buildings	burning	masks	quickly
roar	station	tightly	

A fire erupted last night at the Townville apartment (noun)

_____ _____

_____. Firefighters (adverb) _____

responded to the call from the emergency operators. They could

_____

hear the (noun) _____ of the fire as they approached.

_____

The firefighters pulled their (noun) _____ over their faces
to protect themselves. They then ran toward the (adjective)

_____ _____

_____ buildings, holding (adverb) _____ to
their hoses. They worked steadily for one hour, and the fire was

_____

extinguished. They returned to the fire (noun) _____
weary but glad that no one had been injured.

Annie Makes a Big Change

SUMMARY In this fiction story, Annie is upset when she finds out that trees are being cut down to make room for new houses. Annie thinks a park should go there. Annie and her mother talk to Mrs. Potter, and together they are able to make a change for the whole community.

LESSON VOCABULARY

annoy	complain	mumbles
P.M.	signature	shrugs

INTRODUCE THE BOOK

INTRODUCE THE TITLE AND AUTHOR Read the title and the author's name with the children. Have them look at the cover illustration. Tell children that Annie is the child in the picture. Point out that she is surrounded by adults who are listening to her, though there is one man walking away. Point out the trees in the background. Ask children to look for other details in the picture. Ask them what change they think Annie is going to make.

BUILD BACKGROUND Have children talk about some ways they would like to make their neighborhood a better place in which to live. Ask: What is one thing you would like to change in your neighborhood? How do you think you might be able to make that change? Who would you need to ask for help?

PREVIEW/USE TEXT FEATURES Have children look through the book. Have them notice the diagram on page 10. Guide them to see that this diagram lists steps for making a change. Have children look at page 11 and ask what they think Annie is doing in that picture. After looking at all of the pictures, have children predict what kind of change Annie will make.

READ THE BOOK

SET PURPOSE Have children set a purpose for reading *Annie Makes a Big Change*. Remind children of what was discussed during previewing. Suggest that they read to find out if their predictions about the change Annie makes are correct.

STRATEGY SUPPORT: VISUALIZE Tell children that good readers form pictures in their minds as they read. After reading page 4, ask the children to close their eyes. Reread the page aloud to them. Ask them to form pictures in their minds as you read and share with the class what they visualized.

COMPREHENSION QUESTIONS

PAGE 5 Why were the trees by the stream being cut down? *(to clear the land for new houses)*

PAGE 8 Does Mrs. Potter agree with Annie? How do you know? *(Yes. She smiles and says, "Then we need to get to work.")*

PAGE 10 What are the four steps for making a big change? *(1. See and write about a problem. 2. Get signatures. 3. Show public officials your petition. 4. Public officials decide what to do next.)*

PAGE 15 Why do you think the author decided to have a child as his main character, instead of an adult? *(Possible responses: to make the story more interesting to kids; to show that kids can make changes too)*

REVISIT THE BOOK

READER RESPONSE

1. Responses will vary but should show understanding of an effect.
2. Responses will vary but should include reference to text or illustrations.
3. It means to bother them.
4. Responses will vary but should show understanding of cause and effect.

EXTEND UNDERSTANDING Have children look at the illustrations in the book to see how Annie's feelings change throughout the story. Say: Look at page 3. How is Annie feeling? How can you tell? How does she look on page 5? on page 6? on page 12? How do the pictures on pages 14 and 15 let us know how Annie is feeling? Discuss with children how illustrations can often give us as much information as the text.

RESPONSE OPTIONS

WRITING Ask children to write a few sentences about a change that they would like to make in their school. They can then draw pictures of what they want to change and write the steps they would need to take to make the change happen.

SCIENCE CONNECTION

Using age-appropriate books, have children research how trees help keep our air clean. Ask them to draw a diagram showing how trees take in carbon dioxide and give off oxygen. Then, have children share their diagrams with the class, and post the diagrams on a bulletin board.

Skill Work

TEACH/REVIEW VOCABULARY

Have children make vocabulary cards. Ask them to draw a picture for each vocabulary word to help them remember the meanings.

ELL Write vocabulary words on pairs of index cards. Invite children to play a memory game. As they turn over the cards, have the children read the words aloud.

TARGET SKILL AND STRATEGY

CAUSE AND EFFECT Help children recognize *cause-and-effect* relationships that are not signaled by clue words such as *because*. Draw children's attention to the text on page 4. Ask: What caused Annie to be upset? (*The trees were being cut down*) What is the effect of Anna going to talk to Mrs. Potter? (*They started a petition.*) Clarify the skill by prompting children to reword the text using the word *because* to connect the causes and effects.

VISUALIZE Remind children that to *visualize* is to form pictures in their minds. As children read page 4, ask: What pictures do you see in your mind? Ask children to be as detailed as possible.

ADDITIONAL SKILL INSTRUCTION

AUTHOR'S PURPOSE Recall with children that an *author's purpose* is the reason an author writes something. Explain that there are four main reasons for writing: to inform, to express, to entertain, and to persuade. Invite children to discuss why the author may have chosen to write this book.

Name _____

Cause and Effect

Fill in the numbered boxes to tell what happened or why it happened.

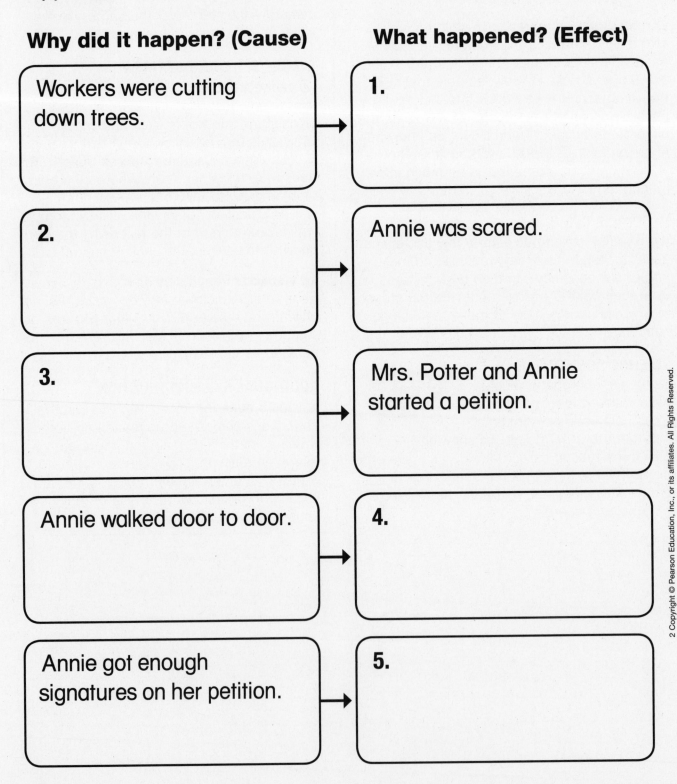

Why did it happen? (Cause)   **What happened? (Effect)**

Why did it happen? (Cause)	What happened? (Effect)
Workers were cutting down trees.	**1.**
2.	Annie was scared.
3.	Mrs. Potter and Annie started a petition.
Annie walked door to door.	**4.**
Annie got enough signatures on her petition.	**5.**

Name _____

Vocabulary

Use the vocabulary words to write three or four sentences about a change you would like to make in your school. Try to use as many vocabulary words as possible. Underline the vocabulary words in each sentence.

Example: He <u>shrugs</u> and <u>mumbles</u> as he writes his <u>signature</u>.

Words to Know
annoy   complain   mumbles   P.M.   signature   shrugs

_____

- -

_____

- -

_____

- -

_____

- -

_____

- -

_____

- -

_____

- -

_____

Hubert and Frankie

SUMMARY This fiction book tells the story of the Kent family's new puppy, Frankie. Frankie has trouble listening and behaving, so Hubert, the older family dog, helps him learn.

LESSON VOCABULARY

chased	chewing
dripping	grabbed
practice	treat
wagged	

INTRODUCE THE BOOK

INTRODUCE THE TITLE AND AUTHOR Discuss with children the title and the author of *Hubert and Frankie*. Invite children to look at the cover illustration and describe what they see happening. Ask: What is the puppy doing? Do you think the woman is happy about this? How do you know? Who do you think Hubert and Frankie are?

BUILD BACKGROUND Engage children in a discussion of pets and puppies. Invite those who have puppies, dogs, or other pets at home to share their experiences. Encourage them to describe both good and bad things about having pets.

PREVIEW Have children preview the book, looking at the illustrations. Ask children to describe what they see happening on each page and to predict what the text might be about. Ask: What is the puppy doing here? How do you think the family will feel about his behavior? What do you think the older dog thinks about the puppy?

READ THE BOOK

SET PURPOSE Based on your discussion of the cover illustration, encourage children to set a purpose for reading this book. Ask: What is happening on the cover of the book? Why do you think the puppy is digging? Suggest that children read on to find out.

STRATEGY SUPPORT: PRIOR KNOWLEDGE Encourage children to use prior knowledge throughout their reading. As they read, remind them of the information they shared before reading and have them connect this information to the text. Ask: What do you already know about puppies that would explain why Frankie likes chasing the cat and chewing on shoes? What do you know about older dogs that tells you why Hubert behaves better than Frankie?

COMPREHENSION QUESTIONS

PAGE 3 Why do you think Hubert thought Frankie was trouble? *(because Frankie misbehaved by chasing the cat and chewing on shoes)*

PAGE 7 What does Hubert remember? Why does this make him think he might be able to help? *(He remembers how hard it was to listen and behave when he was a puppy. He can help because he remembers and understands how hard it is for Frankie.)*

PAGE 10 Why do you think it is fun for Frankie to practice with Hubert? *(Possible response: because he is learning from another dog)*

PAGE 12 Why does Frankie stop reaching for the hamburger when Madeline says, "No, Frankie!"? *(Because he has learned his name and how to listen.)*

PAGE 15 Why do you think Frankie still can't resist chasing the cat once in a while? *(Possible response: It takes a long time to learn, and he is still a puppy.)*

REVISIT THE BOOK

READER RESPONSE

1. Theme: Learning the rules. Plot/events: Kents get Frankie; Frankie misbehaves; Hubert teaches Frankie the rules; Madeline's hamburger falls to the ground; the two dogs show their owners what they have worked on; everyone is happy and the two dogs get a treat.

2. Answers will vary, but children should be encouraged to use prior knowledge.

3. *run, walk, rush, race, crawl, etc.*

4. Possible response: Frankie worked harder, because he learned all the rules.

EXTEND UNDERSTANDING Remind children that a character is a person or an animal in a story. Have them describe what they know about Hubert based on what they've read in the story. Ask: Does Hubert like Frankie? What tells you this? Why do you think Hubert helps Frankie? Why and how do you think Hubert became such a well-behaved dog? What do you think he was like as a puppy?

RESPONSE OPTIONS

WRITING Ask children to write a short paragraph about the story from Frankie's point of view. Have them think about how Frankie might feel when he is told "No!" and whether or not he misbehaves on purpose. Encourage children to consider these questions: Why do you think Frankie behaves the way he does? Do you think he does it on purpose? If he could talk to the family, what do you think he would say?

SOCIAL STUDIES CONNECTION

Engage children in a discussion of social responsibilities. Ask children to describe what things they can to do at home or school to show that they are responsible. These can include doing chores, not interrupting others, not pushing on the playground, completing schoolwork, and so on. Write the title *Our Responsibilities* on a large piece of paper and list the children's ideas to post in the classroom.

Skill Work

TEACH/REVIEW VOCABULARY

Have children write down each of the vocabulary words and discuss the definitions. Assist the children in writing sentences using each of the words.

ELL Use pantomime to help children understand the meanings of the vocabulary words. Children may enjoy taking turns acting out the words for each other.

TARGET SKILL AND STRATEGY

PLOT AND THEME Prior to reading, tell the children that every story has a "big idea" called a *theme.* Explain that this big idea is what the story is all about. It might be something the characters learn or even something that we've learned about from reading the story. As they read, encourage children to take note of the different events that can help tell us what the big idea of the story might be. After reading, use the first Reader Response question to review and discuss the theme and main events in the book.

PRIOR KNOWLEDGE Before reading, use your discussion of puppies and other pets to encourage children to activate their existing knowledge of the subject. Ask: What do you know about puppies and dogs that might help you better understand this story? What did you know about puppies that helped you understand what is happening on the cover of the book?

ADDITIONAL SKILL INSTRUCTION

COMPARE AND CONTRAST Remind children what it means to compare and contrast, then ask them to describe ways that Hubert and Frankie are the same and how they are different. Encourage children to name both physical characteristics as well as how the two dogs behave. Use a Venn diagram to help children organize their ideas.

Name _____

Plot and Theme

Hubert and Frankie is all about learning the rules. Circle the three events from the story that best relate to learning and the rules. Then write "beginning," "middle," or "end" next to the circled events to tell when they happened in the story.

_____

_____

1. Hubert taught Frankie to listen and what the words *no* and *stop* meant.

_____

2. Madeline tried and tried to teach Frankie to sit, but he would not listen.

_____

3. Hubert had lived with the Kent family for a long time and Frankie was the new puppy.

_____

4. Hubert thought Frankie was trouble.

_____

5. Frankie showed the Kents that he knew how to sit.

Name _____

Vocabulary

Choose a word from the box that best fits in each sentence.

> **Words to Know**
>
> chased   chewing   dripping   grabbed
> practice   treat   wagged

1. To show he was happy, Frankie _____ his tail.

2. Frankie _____ the baseball glove.

3. Frankie liked _____ on bones.

4. After splashing in the puddle, Frankie was _____ wet.

5. Hubert helped Frankie _____ how to behave.

6. Both Frankie and Hubert got a _____ when they were good.

7. Frankie still _____ the cat sometimes.

Everyone Can Make A Difference!

⌕ CHARACTER AND SETTING
⌕ TEXT STRUCTURE

SUMMARY This nonfiction book describes how children can work together to protect the environment. It supports and extends the lesson concept of being a good friend and neighbor.

LESSON VOCABULARY

adventure	climbed
clubhouse	exploring
greatest	truest
wondered	

INTRODUCE THE BOOK

INTRODUCE THE TITLE AND AUTHOR Discuss with children the title and author of *Everyone Can Make A Difference!* Explain that social studies includes learning about how people work to change the world. Ask: How might this book relate to social studies?

BUILD BACKGROUND Have children share their experiences of helping out at home. Ask and discuss: How could you help your neighborhood?

PREVIEW/TAKE A PICTURE WALK Have children look at the pictures, headings, bulleted list, and labels in the book before reading. Discuss how the headings help them to read this book by showing when a new topic begins. Ask: Why are there labels in the picture on page 6?

READ THE BOOK

SET PURPOSE Have children set a purpose for reading *Everyone Can Make A Difference!* Remind children of what they discussed in building background. Ask: What might you learn from reading this book?

STRATEGY SUPPORT: TEXT STRUCTURE Explain that *text structure* is the way a story is organized. While the children read, ask them to focus on the headings in the text. Tell them that these will help them better understand each section and keep track of the overall order of the book.

COMPREHENSION QUESTIONS

PAGE 4 Why is it important to protect the environment? (*Possible response: We need it to live.*)

PAGE 8 Why might stray dogs be more likely to get rabies than pet dogs? (*They have no one to care for them.*)

PAGE 12 Why does the author include a picture of a contract? (*Possible response: She wants you to believe it is very important to keep a promise about protecting the environment.*)

PAGE 15 Why should your friends be ready to help you? (*Possible response: They care about me, so they care about what I care about.*)

REVISIT THE BOOK

READER RESPONSE

1. Possible response: Character: the students Setting: wetlands, vets office, roadsides, and school.
2. Possible response: Beginning: making a difference. Middle: making less waste, helping animals, protecting habitats. End: teaching others.
3. Responses will vary but should reflect correct use of the words *greatest* and *truest*.
4. Possible response: I would like to go rock climbing.

EXTEND UNDERSTANDING Point out the bullets on page 15. Ask: What are these for? Guide children to see how they set apart items in a list.

RESPONSE OPTIONS

WRITING Have children write a short letter to the editor about an environmental problem in their community and what should be done about it.

SOCIAL STUDIES CONNECTION

Have small groups of children work together to draw up a plan for helping the EPA in their community. Suggest that they have an adult help them review the EPA's "For Kids" page at www.epa.gov for ideas.

Skill Work

TEACH/REVIEW VOCABULARY

Give children cards with vocabulary words written on them. Write the following on the board, and read them aloud: *searching, best, questioned, meeting place, most dependable, trip, went up.* Ask children to show the vocabulary word that matches each.

ELL Use pictures, objects, or gestures to explain these words from the book: *litterbug, wetlands, vet, vaccination, reusable, contract, aluminum.*

TARGET SKILL AND STRATEGY

CHARACTER AND SETTING Remind children that *characters* are the people in the story and the *setting* is when and where they story takes place. Have children identify the settings in the second chapter of the story. Ask children how the characters felt from one year to the next. (*Hopeful, happy, or successful*)

TEXT STRUCTURE After children have finished reading, write the story headings on the board and have the children write the story headings on a piece of paper. Read each heading and briefly discuss what each section was about. Ask students to use words such as *first, then, next,* and *last* as you move through the book.

ADDITIONAL SKILL INSTRUCTION

DRAW CONCLUSIONS Tell children that as they read, they can use what they have read and seen and what they know to figure out more about what happens in the book. Model: On page 6, I read that the students added bat boxes to attract bats. I know that most people don't like bats. I think that bats must be good for the environment. After page 10, ask: Where did all the garbage come from?

Character and Setting

Read each sentence below.
Then circle the answer that best completes each sentence.

1. The story happened

   a. in 1920   **b.** in present day   **c.** at 1 p.m.

2. The children practiced recycling and reducing at school and

   a. at the doctors   **b.** at the vet   **c.** along the roads

3. The students who volunteered to work with at the animal center felt

   a. worried   **b.** confused   **c.** honored

4. Cans for Kids is a group of

   a. mothers and   **b.** teachers and   **c.** adults
      daughters   students   and kids

5. Write a sentence about another way you can help your community.

Name_____

Vocabulary

Write a word from the box that best fits into each sentence.

Words to Know			
adventure	climbed	clubhouse	exploring
greatest	truest	wondered	

1. We built a _____ for our bird club to meet in.

2. The person who picked up the most litter did the
_____
_____ job.

3. We _____ how many cans we collected.

4. They _____ the ladder to the treehouse.

5. Your _____ friends will help you keep the park clean.

6. Helping on a recyling project can be a big
_____ .

7. _____ new places can be fun.

Freda the Signmaker

SUMMARY Freda volunteers to make signs for the town of Midvale, but she forgets to bring along a list of what the signs are supposed to say. This fantasy selection tells the story of what happens when we are forgetful and not responsible for our jobs.

LESSON VOCABULARY

afternoon	blame
idea	important
signmaker	townspeople

INTRODUCE THE BOOK

INTRODUCE THE TITLE AND AUTHOR Discuss with children the title and the author of *Freda the Signmaker*. Invite them to look at the cover illustration. Based on the title and the illustration, ask them to say what they think the book will be about.

BUILD BACKGROUND Invite children to tell about times they have forgotten things. Remind children that we all forget things from time to time, but that it is important to learn ways to help ourselves remember better.

PREVIEW/TAKE A PICTURE WALK As children preview the book, have them notice the illustrations and the feature on page 16. Ask them to make predictions about what the story will be about, based on these text features.

READ THE BOOK

SET PURPOSE Have children set a purpose for reading *Freda the Signmaker*. Children's interest in seeing what happens when people become forgetful and their interest in learning how to correct mistakes should guide this purpose.

STRATEGY SUPPORT: INFERRING Tell children to look for facts in the text and combine them with what they already know, to learn something new. Model by reading page 5. Say: I read that Freda did not have her list. I know that she is forgetful. I can infer that Freda will make mistakes on the signs.

COMPREHENSION QUESTIONS

PAGE 3 What was Freda's problem? *(She was very forgetful.)*

PAGE 5 What did Freda forget? How did she decide to solve that problem? *(She forgot the list of signs; she thought she could remember them.)*

PAGE 9 How did people respond when the park ranger told them to stay on the paths? *(Possible response: They ignored her and did what the sign said.)*

PAGE 10 What were dogs trained to do at the Acme Watchdog School? *(bark)*

PAGE 13 What did Freda do when Mayor Martin asked her if she used the list he gave her for the signs? *(Possible response: She told him the truth, that she had forgotten the list.)*

REVISIT THE BOOK

READER RESPONSE

1. Responses will vary but answers should be supported with details from the story.
2. Possible response: I know Freda is forgetful and feels guilty for forgetting her list. I can infer that Freda will remember her list next time.
3. Mayor Martin, the park ranger
4. Possible response: She could have gone back for the list.

EXTEND UNDERSTANDING Have children describe their favorite illustrations in the book. Then have them review the feature on page 16. Invite them to say whether they think the information presented in the feature is a realistic story or a fantasy. Challenge them to say why.

RESPONSE OPTIONS

WRITING Have children take a walk to see signs in and around school. Invite them to imagine what would happen if the signmaker was as forgetful as Freda. Invite children to make temporary replacement signs that read the opposite of the originals (e.g., Not the Principal's Office; Not Welcome). Ask: How would these mistakes affect the school day?

ELL Invite students to read signs in the classroom. Explain that signs usually have few words to tell their messages.

SOCIAL STUDIES CONNECTION

Ask children to talk about what happens when people are not responsible on the job. Imagine what would happen if various community and school helpers did not do their jobs or forgot what they needed to do (e.g., the librarian did not take care of the books, the custodian did not clean the school). Children may wish to make their own "books" that show what would happen in their home, school, or community if people forgot to do their jobs. They can illustrate their books and make an exhibit.

Skill Work

TEACH/REVIEW VOCABULARY

Create a vocabulary word wall by printing each word on a sentence strip card and placing cards backwards in a pocket chart. Choose one word at a time to display, define, and discuss. Tell children one page number where each word appears. Invite children to skim the text to locate each word in context.

TARGET SKILL AND STRATEGY

MAIN IDEA After reading, discuss the main idea of the story with the children. Tell the children that the main idea is the most important idea in the story and the details are small pieces of information that support the main idea. Ask children to name details from the story and write them on the board. Have children work in pairs to determine the main idea of the story then discuss the supporting details.

INFERRING After reading the story, remind children that inferring is using the facts in the text and what they already know to learn something new. Ask: If Freda remembered her list would the community have run into these problems? What details lead you to this conclusion?

ADDITIONAL SKILL INSTRUCTION

THEME Explain that when authors write realistic stories or fantasies, they usually want to express a big idea. To understand the big idea, or *theme*, of this story, invite children to ask themselves questions such as, "What did the characters learn?" After they read, give them this question frame: "What does this story teach you about _____?" Challenge them to complete the question and answer the question to help them arrive at their interpretation of the big idea.

Name _____

Main Idea

Read the paragraph below.

> Freda was very forgetful. She was asked to paint signs around town. Before starting, Freda realized she forgot the list of what she needed to paint. She did her best to remember what the list said. All of the signs were wrong. This confused the townspeople and made problems in town. Freda fixed the signs and always read her list before she painted!

Write the main idea of the paragraph below.

_____

_____

_____

_____

_____

_____

_____

_____

Name _____

Vocabulary

Read the words in the first column below.
Then read the words in the second column.
Draw lines to connect the words and make compound words found
in the story.

1. sign   **a.** people

2. towns   **b.** noon

3. after   **c.** maker

4. Write a sentence with the word *blame*.

----

5. Write a sentence with the words *idea* and *important*.

Women Play Baseball

SUMMARY This nonfiction text explores the history of women in baseball, from the late 1800s to present day.

LESSON VOCABULARY

bases	cheers
field	plate
sailed	threw

INTRODUCE THE BOOK

INTRODUCE THE TITLE AND AUTHOR Discuss with children the title and the author of *Women Play Baseball*. Based on the title, ask children what they think this book will be about. Also call attention to the genre on the back cover of the book. Have children explain what nonfiction means and guide them in determining that this book will probably contain historical and factual information about women in baseball.

BUILD BACKGROUND Engage children in a discussion of baseball. Ask: Who likes baseball? Do you prefer to watch or to play baseball? Who are some of your favorite baseball players? Do you know of any women baseball players?

PREVIEW/TAKE A PICTURE WALK Have children preview the book, looking at the pictures. Point out the photographs on pages 4–5 and 9. Ask: Who or what do you think these groups of women are? Why are they wearing uniforms? Also call attention to the three photographs on pages 12–13 and encourage children to describe what is happening. Ask: How do these three photographs go together? What is happening? Which photograph shows what happens first? second? third?

READ THE BOOK

SET PURPOSE Model for children how to set a purpose for reading. Say: "These three photographs on pages 12 and 13 are very interesting. I can tell that they go together, and I am curious to learn more about what happened." Have children choose their own interesting photographs from the book and explain why they would like to learn more about them.

STRATEGY SUPPORT: MONITOR AND CLARIFY Remind children that good readers stop and clarify what they are reading if they don't understand. Ask children: Who is the story about? Where does the story take place? Over what years does the story take place?

ELL Visualizing is an important tool in comprehension. To this end, it may be easier for English language learners to describe their mental pictures in their native languages.

COMPREHENSION QUESTIONS

PAGE 3 How long have women been playing baseball? *(more than 100 years)*

PAGE 5 Why was the All-American Girls Professional Baseball League started in 1943? *(because many men went off to war and most women did not go)*

PAGE 11 Even after the women's professional softball league ended, how do we know that softball was still popular? *(It was part of the Pan-American Games in 1979; colleges formed teams; it became an Olympic sport in 1996.)*

PAGE 15 The author says that baseball is not just for boys and men. How do we know this? *(Responses may vary but should come from information provided in the text. Women have been playing baseball for a long time, and there are many examples of women being involved in this sport.)*

REVIST THE BOOK

READER RESPONSE

1. Use chart to organize differences. Prior to 1948, women's baseball was getting increasingly popular and the AAGPBL was formed; after 1948, attendance dropped and the league soon ended. Girls and women continue to play baseball and softball.
2. Possible response: glove is blocking the plate and player
3. Possible response: moved quickly
4. For the first time, women played professional baseball.

EXTEND UNDERSTANDING Call children's attention to the captions next to the photographs. Read each caption as you look at the corresponding photograph. Discuss how the caption helps us understand what is happening in the photo, and how it helps us understand the rest of the text. Say: "Pages 4 and 5 talk about the first women's baseball teams. This photograph actually shows us a team from the early 1900s. We know this because the caption says so. Would it be as clear that this is a team from the early 1900s if we didn't have the caption?" Continue in a similar manner with the other photographs and captions in the book.

RESPONSE OPTIONS

WRITING Have children make a time line of the events surrounding women in baseball using the information provided in the text. Help children gather this information from the text, and show them how to organize the dates along their time lines. Guide them in using the book to write a short sentence or two for each date. Children can then illustrate their time lines.

SOCIAL STUDIES CONNECTION

Provide children with additional information on women in sports. Encourage them to use the library or the Internet to research women's involvement in other sports that interest them. Then have children share the information they've learned with the rest of the class.

Skill Work

TEACH/REVIEW VOCABULARY

Have children practice looking up the definitions of the vocabulary words in the glossary and then write the words and definitions on their own papers. For extra practice, help children think of and write short sentences using the words.

TARGET SKILL AND STRATEGY

COMPARE AND CONTRAST Remind the children what it means to *compare* and *contrast*. Have children look at the uniforms the women are wearing in the photographs on pages 4–5 and 8–9. Have children describe how these uniforms are the same and different. Use a Venn diagram to record children's observations.

MONITOR AND CLARIFY Tell children to pace their reading to see relationships between facts and ideas in the text. Identifying cause-and-effect relationships without signal words can be challenging at their level. Help children by reminding them to read slowly and to look at the illustrations and photographs to clarify their understanding.

ADDITIONAL SKILL INSTRUCTION

CAUSE AND EFFECT Turn to page 9 and read the text out loud with the children. Then guide children in determining what happened and why. Say: "Here it says that by 1954, only five teams could finish their season and the women's league ended soon after that. Why?" Help children identify the events (or causes) that led to the end of the All-American Girls Professional Baseball League. List these on the board or have children use a graphic organizer with arrows indicating how one event led to another. *(Women's baseball became less popular, people stopped going to games; no money from ticket sales, teams couldn't pay players; teams went out of business, league ended.)*

Name _____

Compare and Contrast

Use the chart below to compare and contrast baseball with another sport, like basketball, soccer, or football. Write the name of the sport you choose on the line provided.

Baseball	Both	_____

Name _____

Vocabulary

Pretend that you are playing baseball. Write a short story using each of the words in the word box once. The story has been started for you.

Words to Know
athlete   bases   cheers   field   plate   sailed   threw

When I first got to the game, I heard all of the loud

_____

_____ from the crowd.

_____

_____

_____

_____

_____

_____

_____

_____

_____

American Revolution Heroes

⊙ **AUTHOR'S PURPOSE**
⊙ **SUMMARIZE**

SUMMARY Many people helped the United States gain its independence from Great Britain, including Benjamin Franklin, George Washington, Margaret Corbin, and Dicey Langston. Everyone helped in different ways, from eliciting aid from France to leading the army; from firing cannons to warning of British attack. Today, we celebrate the birth of America every year on the Fourth of July.

LESSON VOCABULARY

America	birthday	flag
freedom	nickname	stars
stripes		

INTRODUCE THE BOOK

INTRODUCE THE TITLE AND AUTHOR Ask children to identify the book title, as well as the author, on the cover of the book. Read both with the class. Encourage children to describe the image they see on the cover, and have children share ideas about what this illustration reminds them of. Write children's ideas on the board.

BUILD BACKGROUND Write the words *American Revolution* on the board, and ask children what these words mean to them. Explain that the American Revolution led to the United States becoming an independent country, free from English rule. Encourage children to share what they know about the American Revolution.

PREVIEW/TAKE A PICTURE WALK Ask children to explain what they notice about the pictures. Confirm that the pictures show people or events from long ago. Allow children to identify any individuals who they recognize. For example, some children might be familiar with images of Ben Franklin or George Washington. Let children predict what they might learn, based on these illustrations.

READ THE BOOK

SET PURPOSE Work with children to set a purpose for reading *American Revolution Heroes*. Remind children that long ago, America was ruled by Great Britain. Speculate with children who might have helped America achieve independence. As they read, encourage children to look for several people who helped America become independent.

STRATEGY SUPPORT: SUMMARIZE Ask children to practice summarizing by telling about a conflict they had and how they solved it. Remind children that they are only going to tell the most important idea about their conflict.

COMPREHENSION QUESTIONS

PAGE 4 What was the main problem between Great Britain and the Thirteen Colonies? *(The colonists did not want to pay taxes to Great Britain.)*

PAGE 8 What job did George Washington have during the American Revolution? *(He was not President, but he was in charge of the army during the American Revolution.)*

PAGE 14 Why would it be important for the United States to have a flag? *(Each country has its own flag. Having a flag during the American Revolution showed the world that the United States was determined to be its own country.)*

REVISIT THE BOOK

READER RESPONSE

1. Possible response: The author wanted to teach us about our country's history.
2. Events: American Revolution; Battle of Yorktown; The Fourth of July. Heroes: "Daring Dicey" Langston; Benjamin Franklin; Sybil Ludington; George Washington; Deborah Sampson
3. Possible response: The Fourth of July is the day that America declared its independence from Britain and was born.
4. Possible response: On this map of 1775, only thirteen states are identified. Today, we have fifty states.

EXTEND UNDERSTANDING Encourage children to extend their understanding of the text by looking at the illustrations and captions. For example, have children turn to page 9, and ask them to explain how the photograph and caption provide additional information.

RESPONSE OPTIONS

WRITING Invite children to consider who they would like to learn more about—Benjamin Franklin, George Washington, Margaret Corbin, or Dicey Langston. Ask children to write a few sentences about why they would like to learn more about this person.

WORD WORK Write the word *revolution* on the board. Ask a volunteer to look up the word in a dictionary and present its meanings. Discuss how in this book, *revolution* refers to the action of people wanting to change a government or a leader. Ask if *American Revolution* is a good term to identify the years when America fought to be free of English rule. Encourage children to explain their ideas.

SOCIAL STUDIES CONNECTION

Talk with children about why the people in this book are considered heroes. Then ask children to think about other people they consider heroes. Encourage children to draw a picture of a hero and write a few sentences about why that person is a hero.

Skill Work

TEACH/REVIEW VOCABULARY

Write the word *America* in the center of a word web. In the surrounding circles, write *flag, stars, stripes, freedom,* and *birthday.* Encourage children to explain how each word relates to America.

ELL Help English language learners recognize smaller words in *birthday (birth* and *day), freedom (free),* and *nickname (name).* Write each smaller word on an index card. Discuss the meanings of the smaller words, and then talk about how knowing the meanings of the smaller words contributes to understanding the vocabulary words.

TARGET SKILL AND STRATEGY

AUTHOR'S PURPOSE Review with children that an author usually has a purpose for writing. Ask them to think about the *author's purpose* while reading. This will help them set their own purpose for reading.

SUMMARIZE Tell students to *summarize* something is to give the main idea, or most important, ideas in your own words. After discussing pages 6 and 7, have children work in pairs to summarize the information. Let children know they should tell whom the information is about and what happens. Afterwards, have pairs share and compare the information.

ADDITIONAL SKILL INSTRUCTION

COMPARE AND CONTRAST Share with children that when they *compare and contrast,* they recognize how two things are similar and different. Encourage children to compare and contrast two heroes in this book. You might draw a Venn diagram on the board to aid in making comparisons.

Name _____

Author's Purpose

Read the text below. Then circle the best answer for each question.

> In 1775 America was ruled by Great Britain. Many Americans wanted to be an independent country. Many people were willing to fight for independence including Benjamin Franklin, George Washington, and "Daring Dicey." The American colonies became free from Britain on July 4, 1776.

1. Why did the author write about the American Revolutionary War?

    a. to be cheery   **b.** to teach   **c.** to be smart

2. Why did the author include heroes from the American Revolutionary War?

    a. to show us how people lived in 1774

    b. to convince you to help your country

    c. to help you learn about how America became a free country

3. How does the author want you to feel about the 4th of July?

    a. Proud   **b.** Angry   **c.** Tired

4. Write a sentence that tells what you think about the American Revolutionary War after reading *American Revolution Heroes*.

    _____

    _____

    _____

Name _____

Vocabulary

Read each sentence. Choose a word from the box that best fits the sentence. Write one letter on each line.

> ## Words to Know
>
> | America | birthday | flag | freedom |
> |---------|----------|------|---------|
> | nickname | stars | stripes | |

1. The __ __ __ __ __ on the flag stand for the states.

2. The flag also has thirteen __ __ __ __ __ __ __.

3. The American Revolution was fought for America's __ __ __ __ __ __ __ from English rule.

4. The new country became known as the United States of __ __ __ __ __ __ __.

5. Daring Dicey was the __ __ __ __ __ __ __ __ for Dicey Langston.

A World of Birthdays

DRAW CONCLUSIONS
QUESTIONING

SUMMARY This book shows how children around the world celebrate their birthdays in different ways.

LESSON VOCABULARY

aunt	bank
basket	collects
favorite	present

INTRODUCE THE BOOK

INTRODUCE THE TITLE AND AUTHOR Discuss with children the title and author of *A World of Birthdays*. Based on the title, what do they think they might learn? Do they think the book will be about children's birthdays or grown-ups' birthdays? Why?

BUILD BACKGROUND Invite children to share the ways that they celebrate their birthdays. Present the idea that people in different countries might celebrate their birthdays in different ways. If children have any knowledge of how children from other cultures or in other parts of the world celebrate birthdays, ask them to share the information.

PREVIEW/TAKE A PICTURE WALK Have children preview the book. Are there mostly photos or drawings? Do they think the book will be fiction or nonfiction? Why? Ask them what information they get from the headings on each page (the name of a country.) Go over the map on pages 14 and 15 and point out where the different countries are. Discuss what children think they will learn from the book. Note that the book includes a glossary.

READ THE BOOK

SET PURPOSE Have children set a purpose for reading *A World of Birthdays*. Do they want to get some ideas for their own birthday parties? Do they want to know about the kind of presents children get or what sort of games they play at parties? Have them tell you something they hope to find out by reading this book.

STRATEGY SUPPORT: QUESTIONING Explain to children that there is more than one way to find answers to questions. Some answers can be found right there in the text. Other questions might require children to use what they already know to find the answer. Point out question 1 in Think and Share and ask them how they would find the answers.

COMPREHENSION QUESTIONS

PAGE 4 What do you now know about Aisha? *(Possible responses: She likes to have fun. She is thoughtful toward others.)*

PAGES 6–9 How is the food at Rosa's birthday party different from the food at Ilya's party? *(Possible response: Ilya has birthday pie, Rosa has Three Milk Cake.)*

PAGE 11 What will Victor do with the money he gets for his birthday? *(put it in the bank)*

PAGE 15 What is a reason that so many places celebrate birthdays? *(No matter where they are, people want to show how happy they are that the birthday person was born.)*

120 A World of Birthdays

REVISIT THE BOOK

READER RESPONSE

1. Some of the children get sung to and there is a Tagalog song on page 11.
2. Responses will vary but should include a question and how it helped them understand text.
3. Possible response: My favorite present was my doll, Molly, because my grandpa gave it to me.
4. Possible response: Activity: The Round Loaf Why: It sounds fun!

EXTEND UNDERSTANDING Discuss the photos in the book. Point out that each was chosen to show something important about each of the birthdays. Invite children to reread the text in each section and then tell what other images could have been chosen as photographs.

RESPONSE OPTIONS

WRITING Invite children to think about the ways that birthdays are celebrated around the world. Then, ask them to think of what their perfect birthday celebration would be. Have them write a paragraph about that celebration.

ELL When doing the above writing activity, allow ELL students to orally tell you about their perfect birthday celebration, if they find writing the paragraph too difficult.

SOCIAL STUDIES CONNECTION

In this book, children learned about birthday celebrations in different countries. Suggest children learn more about those countries. They can use classroom books, the library, or the Internet when appropriate. Afterwards, they should share with each other the information they learned.

Skill Work

TEACH/REVIEW VOCABULARY

Point out that some vocabulary words have more than one meaning. Give the four meanings for *present*. (to be accounted for; at this time; a gift; to give) Relate the difference in pronouncing *present* when it means "to give," versus the other definitions. Discuss that the word *bank* can mean a place to keep money or the ground alongside a river or lake. Have children share definitions for the rest of the vocabulary words.

TARGET SKILL AND STRATEGY

DRAW CONCLUSIONS Tell children that they can use what they already know to help them better understand new information. Read pages 4 and 5 together. Ask: Do you think Aisha likes birthday parties? Discuss how the text does not answer this question directly. However, children can use the information that her birthday is Aisha's favorite day of the year, that friends and family are coming to celebrate with her, that she expects to have fun, and that tells what they will eat and do to *draw the conclusion* that Aisha likes birthday parties.

QUESTIONING Remind children that good readers know where to look for answers to questions. Tell them to keep in mind the many strategies for answering questions and to use the one that works best. Review the strategies—Right there, In my head, Author and me, On my own.

ADDITIONAL SKILL INSTRUCTION

COMPARE AND CONTRAST Ask children to tell you what it means to *compare* things. (*tell how two or more things are alike and how they are different*) Ask: What do you think might be compared in the book *Birthdays Around the World*? Make a compare-and-contrast chart with these headings: *Food; Games; Who Comes*. Help children fill the chart in after reading the book.

Name_____

Draw Conclusions

Read *A World of Birthdays*. Write the answers to the questions below.

1. What are important parts of all the birthday celebrations in this book?

_____

_____
_____

_____
_____
----

2. Children in different countries eat different birthday food. What else is different about birthdays around the world?

_____
_____

_____
_____

_____

3. Do you think the children in this book enjoyed their birthday parties? Why or why not?

_____
_____

_____
_____

Name_____

Vocabulary

Unscramble the words and write them in the spaces below.

Words to Know
aunt   bank   basket   collects   favorite   present

1. asbket

_____

- - - - - - - - - - - -

_____

2. eftaivor

_____

- - - - - - - - - - - -

_____

3. nkab

_____

- - - - - - - - - - - -

_____

4. costclle

_____

- - - - - - - - - - - -

_____

5. tuan

_____

- - - - - - - - - - - -

6. prteens

_____

- - - - - - - - - - - -

7. Write a sentence using two or more vocabulary words.

_____

- - - - - - - - - - - -

_____

- - - - - - - - - - - -

_____

- - - - - - - - - - - -

A Cowboy's Life

SUMMARY Eight-year-old Jeannie Grigsby tells about a relative from 150 years ago who was a cowboy. She explains what cowboy life was like and why the cowboy's life changed. Through the experiences of Great-great-great-great-uncle Carl, the reader is transported back to the days of the cowboy.

LESSON VOCABULARY

campfire	cattle	cowboy
galloped	herd	railroad
trails		

INTRODUCE THE BOOK

INTRODUCE THE TITLE AND AUTHOR Point to the book title and author's name, and invite children to read both with you. Then invite children to share their ideas about cowboys, and list their ideas on the board. Encourage children to share ideas about where cowboys worked, what they did, the clothes they wore, and so on.

BUILD BACKGROUND Discuss whether cowboys still work and exist today. Let children offer ideas, then explain that, although cowboys do work today, the main time period for cowboys was about 150 years ago. Prompt students to list modern conveniences that did not exist 150 years ago, such as modes of transportation and machines. Ask: Do you think modern inventions had an effect on the cowboys, their jobs, and their way of life? Why?

PREVIEW Starting with page 3, ask children who the girl in the illustration might be. Ask: Who is the man in the picture frame? Help children recognize this man as they preview the illustrations. Afterward, ask children if they have any new ideas about the girl on page 3 and her relation to the man in the picture frame.

READ THE BOOK

SET PURPOSE Before children begin reading, ask them what they would like to learn about cowboy life. Write children's questions on the board. Repeat the questions so children will be able to recall the questions during reading. Then as they read, tell children to look for the answers to their questions.

STRATEGY SUPPORT: STORY STRUCTURE As children read, identifying the story structure helps them understand how one event leads logically to the next. This also helps them separate the main ideas and events from the supporting details.

COMPREHENSION QUESTIONS

PAGE 3 Why does Jeannie Grigsby tell us about Carl Grigsby? *(She has heard many stories about him. He was a cowboy. She thinks others would like to hear about cowboy life.)*

PAGE 7 What was a trail drive like? Write ideas in a word web. *(center circle: trail drive; outer circles possible responses: 3,000 longhorns; three months on the trail; dusty; stampede)*

PAGE 9 Why did Carl think sitting around the campfire was the best part of the trail drive? *(It was a time to rest, relax, talk, eat, and sing songs.)*

PAGE 11 The days of the big trail drives were over was *what happened*. Why did it happen? *(The railroad came to Texas.)*

REVIST THE BOOK

READER RESPONSE

1. Possible response: First: herded cattle Next: rode on trail drives Last: fixed fences.
2. Responses will vary but should answer questions in sequential order.
3. Possible responses: railroad, campfire, longhorn, sunset, cowhands
4. Responses will vary. Riding a horse should be included, but accept all reasonable answers. Make sure children's answers include support from the text.

EXTEND UNDERSTANDING Using the skill of cause and effect, discuss with children how rodeos grew out of the cowboys' way of life. Help children recognize that many events in rodeos are skills the cowboys often practiced. These practices (why it happened) led to friendly competitions (what happened). And these friendly competitions (why it happened) led to more organized competitions, or rodeos (what happened).

RESPONSE OPTIONS

WRITING Explain to children that Carl kept a journal when he was on a cattle drive. Ask children to each write a few sentences that tell what happens during one day on the trail. Let children illustrate their journal entries.

SCIENCE CONNECTION

Work with children to compare the hot, dry plains of the range to other places in the United States, such as forests, mountains, wetlands, and coasts. You might divide the class into groups, and assign one place to each. Help children find library books about that climate or terrain, and ask them to draw a poster to illustrate it. Display the posters to compare the landscapes.

Skill Work

TEACH/REVIEW VOCABULARY

Ask children to identify which vocabulary word appears in the book title. Encourage children to explain how other vocabulary words might relate to cowboys. Help children form their ideas into sentences. For example: *Cowboys lead herds of cattle. Cowboys sit around campfires at night.*

ELL Write each word on a self-stick note. Work with children to look through the book for pictures that illustrate each word. Place the self-stick notes on the pictures to reinforce meaning. Invite children to say the words as they point to the corresponding images in the illustrations.

TARGET SKILL AND STRATEGY

SEQUENCE Tell children that it is important to keep track of the *sequence* or order of events, when reading. As they read, encourage children to think about what comes first, next and last. Ask: What happened first in the story? Then what happened next? Finally, what happened last?

STORY STRUCTURE Tell children that *structure* of a story is usually arranged in a sequence from beginning, middle, and end, with one event leading to the next. Suggest that children make simple story map of what they read, noting the events in the order in which they happen.

ADDITIONAL SKILL INSTRUCTION

CHARACTER Remind students that a *character* is a person or animal who takes part in the events of a story. Explain that authors let readers know what characters are like by telling what they do, say, or feel. Invite children to think about what Carl is like. Have them look for things he does, says, or feels, as they read.

Name _____

Sequence

Fill in each box using the story *A Cowboy's Life*.

Title	
Characters	**Setting**
Events	
1. First	
2. Next	
3. Then	
4. Last	

Name _____

Vocabulary

Circle the word that best completes the sentence and write it in the space.

Words to Know			
campfire	cattle	cowboy	galloped
herd	railroad	trails	

1. Many cows make up one large _____ .

    campfire   herd

2. The cattle _____ across the dry land.

    galloped   railroad

3. Great Uncle Carl was once a _____ .

    railroad   cowboy

4. The cowboys led the cattle on dusty _____ .

    trails   railroad

5. At night, the cowboys cooked over a _____ .

    campfire   herd

6. The _____ changed the life of the cowboy.

    trails   railroad

Voting Day

SUMMARY Children read about a town that holds a special election to decide whether some unused land should be turned into a park or a parking lot.

LESSON VOCABULARY

microphone   slogan   rallies
speeches   election   assembly

INTRODUCE THE BOOK

INTRODUCE THE TITLE AND AUTHOR Discuss the title and author of *Voting Day*. Based on the title and the illustration on the cover, ask children to describe what they think this book might be about. Ask what the children shown on the cover illustration might be doing.

BUILD BACKGROUND Discuss voting with children. Have children think about a time when they or someone in their family had voted on an important issue.

PREVIEW/TAKE A PICTURE WALK Invite children to take a picture walk to preview the text and illustrations. Discuss the steps the main character takes to get ready for voting day.

READ THE BOOK

SET PURPOSE Have children set a purpose for reading *Voting Day*. Ask them to think about how voting works and what voters should do to prepare for voting.

STRATEGY SUPPORT: PREDICT AND SET PURPOSE Tell children that good readers set their purpose for reading by predicting what will probably happen next. Explain that they look for clues as they read to help them decide what might happen next in the story. Model questions to ask while reading: What is happening? Does this match what I predicted might happen? What changes should I make in my predictions?

COMPREHENSION QUESTIONS

PAGES 3–4 What facts about the unused land are described in this text? (*The town doesn't use it. They want to turn it either into a park or a parking lot. There will be a special election to decide what to do with the land.*)

PAGES 6–7 Which facts does Lucy's class learn about the parks and parking lots in their town? (*There is only one park in town. There are three parking lots in town.*)

PAGES 8–9 What details do Lucy and her friends learn about the parks and parking lots in their town? (*That there were 130 parking spaces for cars. That Shady Park only allowed 25 children at a time.*)

PAGE 10 What are two good things a park would bring? (*more trees, more birds*)

PAGE 12 Why is the children's choice of a slogan a good one? (*it's catchy, it plays on the word "park"*)

REVISIT THE BOOK

THINK AND SHARE

1. There is more space for cars than for children to play in the town; there are three parking lots, the lots have space for 130 cars, the one park only has space for 25 children at a time.

2. Possible response: Yes, they will keep speaking out; they have learned about how they can make a difference, Lucy was successful in talking at the town hall, they made a real difference in the outcome of the election

3. Possible responses: We plan to attend rallies to support more pay for our teachers. Lisa will give a speech as the school assembly. I came up with a clever slogan for Rico's class president campaign.

4. Responses will vary.

EXTEND UNDERSTANDING Explain to children that voting is an important part of being a citizen. Discuss the kinds of important topics and issues that require people to vote. For example, classrooms may vote about special projects or class trips, and towns may vote about whether to give money to help schools.

RESPONSE OPTIONS

SPEAKING Have children work in groups to identify important issues that they think should be voted on. Have volunteers take turns talking about their issues. Encourage children to listen attentively to each speaker and ask questions.

SOCIAL STUDIES CONNECTION

Time For **SOCIAL STUDIES**

Provide a large variety of books about American history for children to look through. Have children choose one book and identify the important issues discussed in the book. Have children explain in writing what these important issues were and how they were resolved.

ELL Provide a web for children. In the center of the web, write *election*. Then have them write examples of what they know about an election. Children could draw what they have seen and write words used in elections in treivr home language next to the English word.

Skill Work

TEACH/REVIEW VOCABULARY

Remind children that when they come to an unfamiliar word, they should look at its sentence and surrounding sentences for clues to its meaning. Direct children to find the word *rallies* on page 3. Ask a volunteer to explain its meaning. Ask what surrounding words or sentences gave clues to the meaning. Repeat for each vocabulary word.

TARGET SKILL AND STRATEGY

FACTS AND DETAILS Remind children that *facts* are pieces of information that can be proven to be true, and *details* are small pieces of information that support a fact. Give children a few sentences that present examples of facts and details. Have them identify the facts and the information that supports the facts.

PREDICT AND SET PURPOSE Remind children that *predicting* is thinking about what will probably happen next. Ask children to discuss the predictions they made before reading *Voting Day*.

ADDITIONAL SKILL INSTRUCTION

SEQUENCE Remind children that a story's *sequence* is how things happen in a certain order. As they read, they should think about what happened first, next, and last in the story. Direct children's attention to the text on page 6 and ask children to identify the first thing that Lucy and her friends decide they need to do before the town hall meeting.

Name_____

Facts and Details

A **fact** is a piece of information that can be proven true. **Details** are pieces of information about a story.

Read the details. Circle the details and underline facts that you find in the following sentences from *Voting Day*.

1. People will vote in a special election two weeks from now.

2. There have been a number of rallies recently.

3. There are three parking lots.

4. There is only one park.

5. A sign at the entrance to the playground read "25 Children Maximum."

_____

6–7. Find two details that can be proven true from *Voting Day*. Write them on the lines below.

_____
- -
_____
- -
_____
- -
_____
- -
_____

Vocabulary

Say each word aloud. Then draw a line between each syllable.

Words to Know		
microphone	slogan	rallies
speeches	election	assembly

1. m i c r o p h o n e

2. e l e c t i o n

3. a s s e m b l y

Choose a word from the box that best completes each sentence.

4. We tried to think of a _____
   to put on the poster.

5. The people held many _____
   all over town.

6. We listened to all of the _____
   before we came to a decision.

Story Prediction from Previewing

Title _____

Read the title and look at the pictures in the story.
What do you think a problem in the story might be?

I think a problem might be _____

_____

_____

After reading _____ ,
draw a picture of one of the problems in the story.

Story Prediction from Vocabulary

Title and Vocabulary Words

Read the title and the vocabulary words.
What do you think this story might be about?

I think this story might be about _____

_____

_____

After reading _____ ,
draw a picture that shows what the story is about.

KWL Chart

Topic _____

What We **K** **now**	**What We** **W** **ant to Know**	**What We** **L** **earned**

Vocabulary Frame

Word

Association or Symbol

Predicted definition: _____

_____

One good sentence:

_____

_____

_____

Verified definition: _____

_____

_____

Another good sentence:

_____

_____

_____

Story Predictions Chart

Title _____

What might happen?	What clues do I have?	What did happen?

Story Sequence A

Title _____

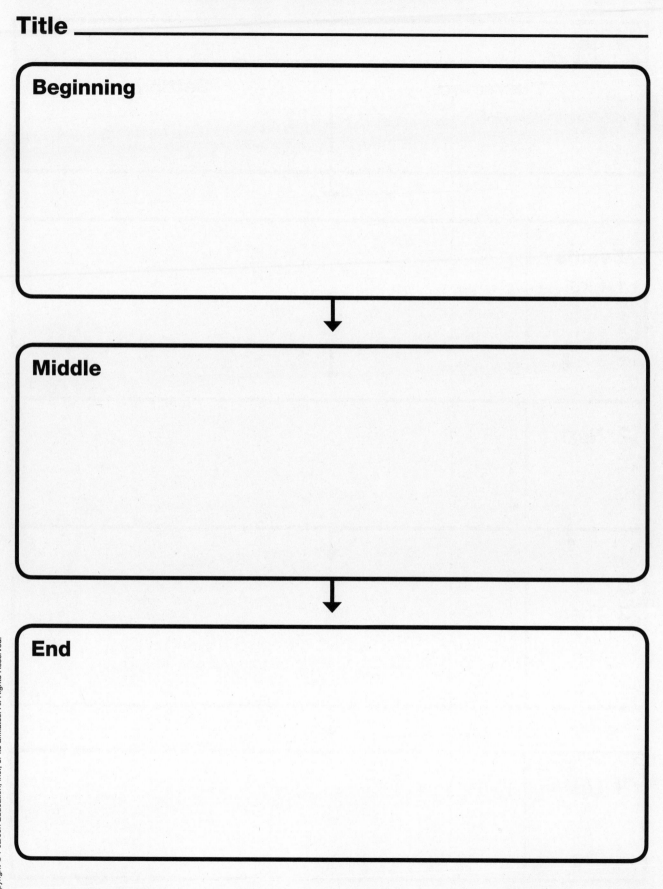

Beginning

Middle

End

Story Sequence B

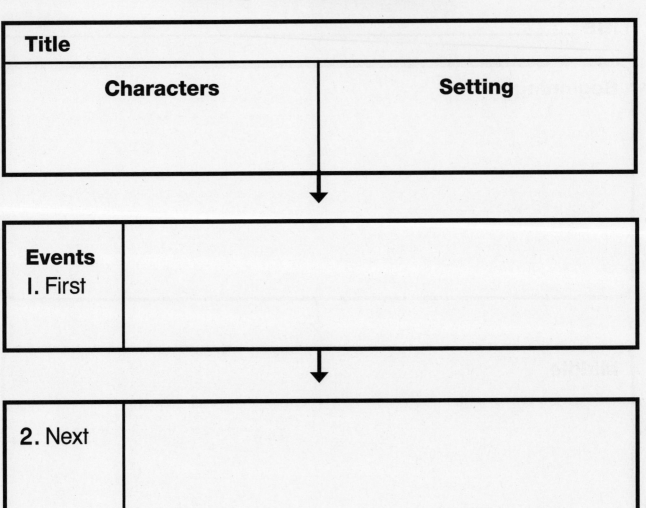

Title	
Characters	**Setting**

Events
1. First

2. Next

3. Then

4. Last

Story Sequence C

Title

Characters

Problem

Events

_____

_____

_____

_____

_____

_____

_____

_____

Solution

Question the Author

Title _____

Author _____ **Page** _____

I. What does the author tell you?	
2. Why do you think the author tells you that?	
3. Does the author say it clearly?	
4. What would make it clearer?	
5. How would you say it instead?	

Story Comparison

Title A _____

_____

Characters

Setting

Events

Title B _____

_____

Characters

Setting

Events

Web

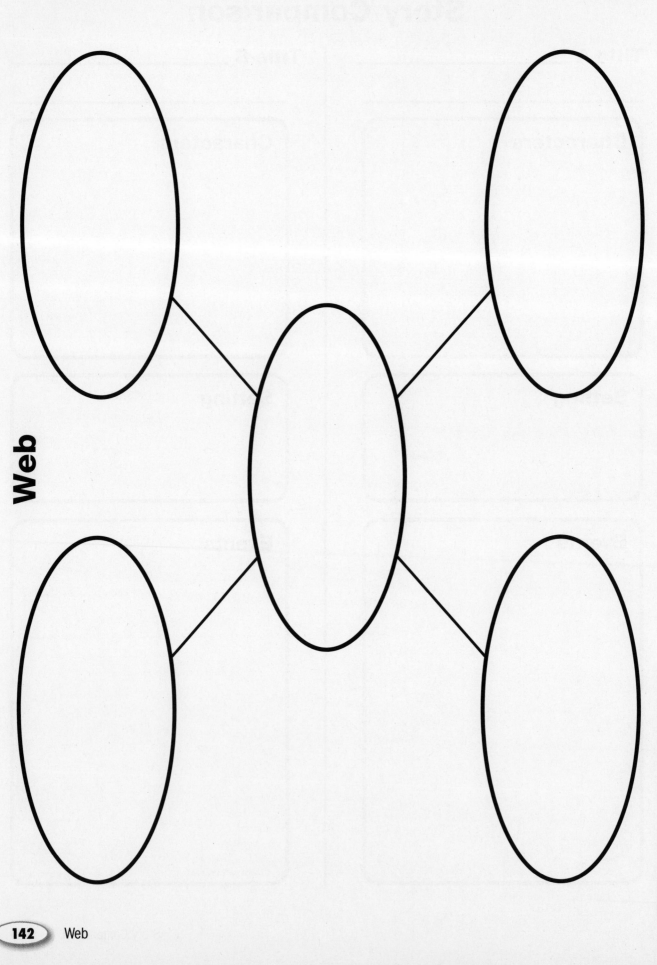

Main Idea

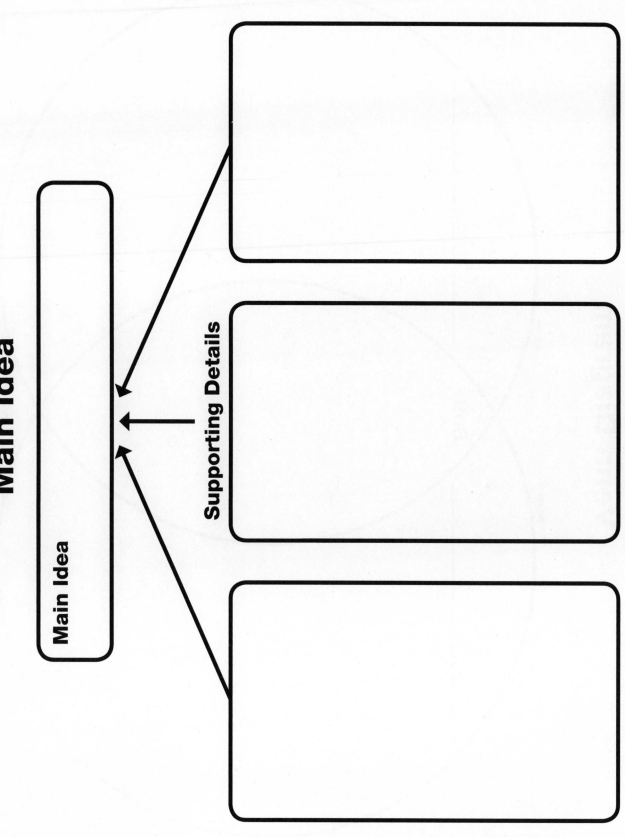

Main Idea

Supporting Details

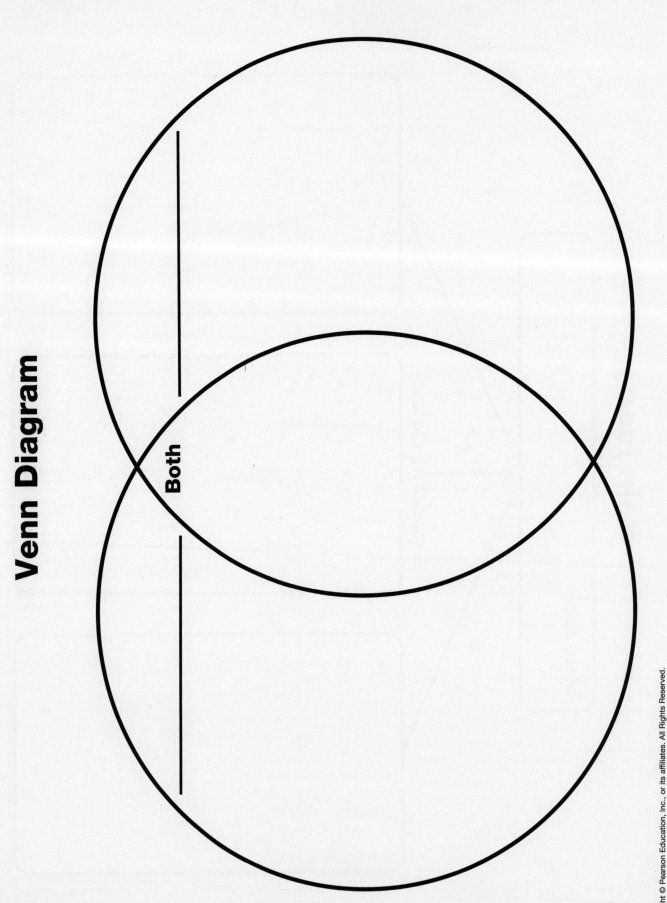

Venn Diagram

Both

Compare and Contrast

Topics

Alike

Different

Cause and Effect

Causes

Effects

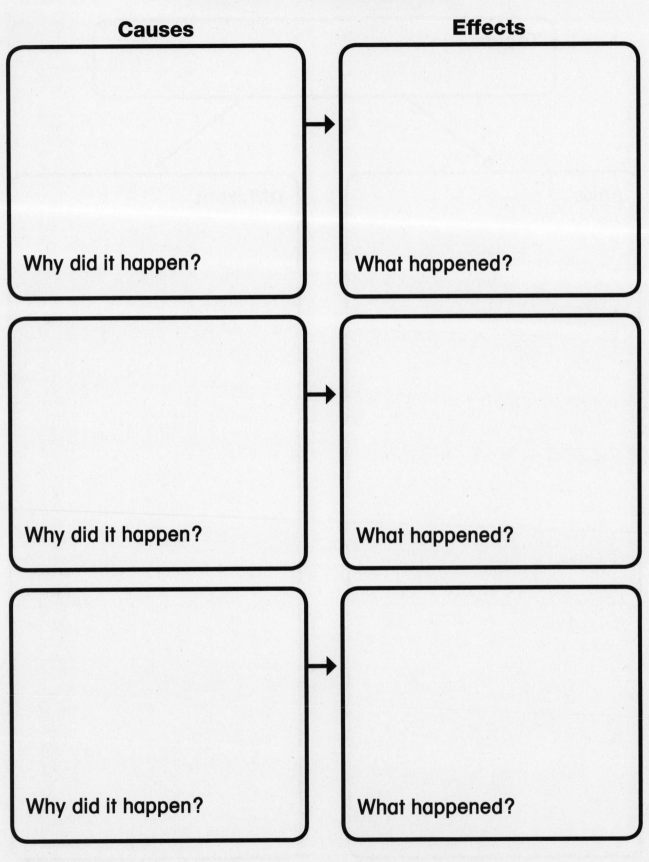

Why did it happen?

What happened?

Why did it happen?

What happened?

Why did it happen?

What happened?

Problem and Solution

Problem

Attempts to Solve the Problem

Solution

Time Line

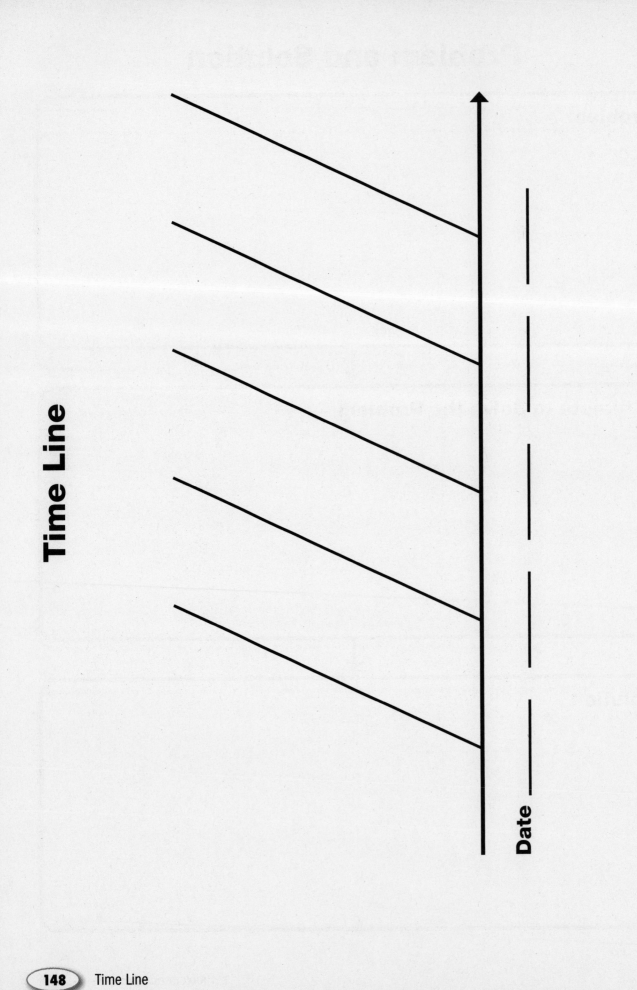

Date _____

Steps in a Process

Process _____

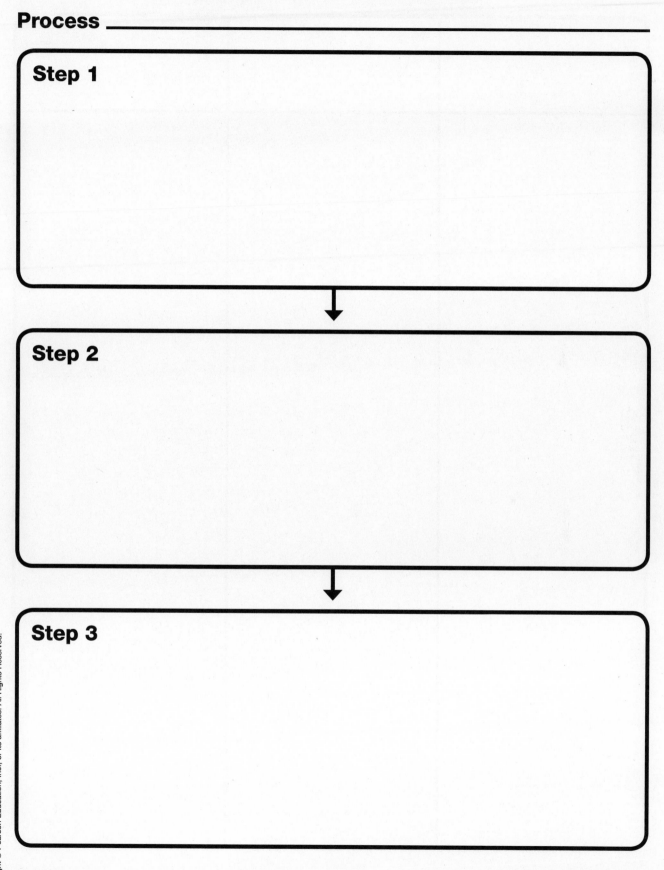

Step 1

Step 2

Step 3

Three-Column Chart

Four-Column Chart

Four-Column Graph

Title _____

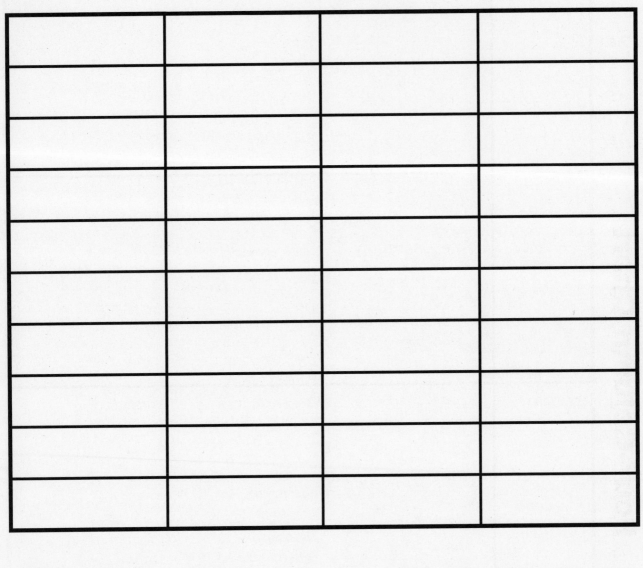

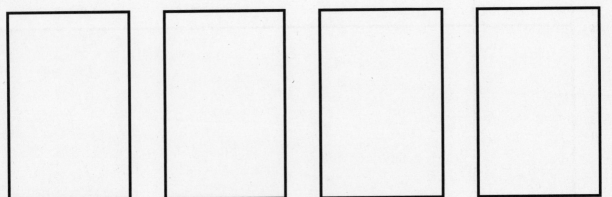

Answer Key

Leveled Reader Practice Pages

The New Kid in Bali p. 14

CHARACTER AND SETTING

Setting: small farms, Bali, island, summer
Character: glad, new kid, adventurous, likes soccer

The New Kid in Bali p. 15 Vocabulary
1. b.
2. c
3. a
4. Possible response: Mom says someone from school can come along.
5. Possible response: I knew my jacket was somewhere in my room.

An Astronaut Space Walk p. 18

MAIN IDEA

Topic: Space walk
Main Idea: There are problems on a space walk.
Supporting Details: There is no air in space. Space junk can hit you.

An Astronaut Space Walk p. 18
1. world
2. machines
3. woman
4. live
5. move
6. everywhere
7. work

Camping at Crescent Lake p. 22

CHARACTER AND SETTING

1. b
2. c
3. a
4. b
5. Possible response: pancakes, the beach, building sand castles

Camping at Crescent Lake p. 23 Vocabulary
1. d
2. c
3. b
4. a
5. bear, straight, mother

Desert Animals p. 26

MAIN IDEA

Main Idea: Desert animals are able to survive in the desert.
Possible responses: Details: Camels: drink once a week, drink 35 gallons of water in six minutes, can drink 35 gallons of water before they are full; Jerboa: never drinks, lives underground, and has strong back legs; Jack Rabbit: hunt in the early evening, stay out of the sun, come out in the early evening; Desert Owl: flutters to cool off, has big eyes to see at night, hunts at night.

Desert Animals p. 27 Vocabulary
1. full
2. eyes
3. early
4. water
5. animals
6. warm

Glooskap and the First Summer: An Algonquin Tale p. 30

FACTS AND DETAILS

1. underline
2. circle
3. circle
4. circle
5. underline
6–7. Possible response: The story of Glooskap is a myth of the Algonquin people. Storytelling has always been important to the Algonquin.

Glooskap and the First Summer: An Algonquin Tale p. 31 Vocabulary

1. learn
2. often
3. gone
4. pieces
5. though
6. very
7. together

Be Ready for an Emergency p. 34

🎯 **CAUSE AND EFFECT**

1. Possible responses: Effect: Go to the nearest counter or desk; Tell and adult you are lost; know your address and phone number.
2. Cause: Getting out of a fire.
3. Effect: Break a window.
4. Cause: Calling 9-1-1 for help.
5. Effect: You learn important safety tips.

Be Ready for an Emergency p. 35 Vocabulary

1. d
2. a
3. b
4. e
5. c
6. f
7. Possible response: I like to listen to birds chirp.

Let's Work Together! p. 38

🎯 **AUTHOR'S PURPOSE**

1. a
2. c
3. c
4. Possible response: I would like to do yard work with my friends.

Let's Work Together! p. 39 Vocabulary

1. b
2. a
3. f
4. c
5. e
6. d
7. i
8. h
9. j
10. g

Farming Families p. 42

🎯 **FACTS AND DETAILS**

1. underline
2. circle
3. underline
4. circle
5. circle
6–7. Responses will vary but should be supported by facts from the story.

Farming Families p. 43 Vocabulary

1. ago
2. enough
3. whole
4. above
5. toward

Possible response: I did not eat enough so I was still hungry.

Growing Up p. 46

🎯 **CAUSE AND EFFECT**

1. Pepper ran after him.
2. Pepper licked Jun's face.
3. Pepper went to dog school.
4. Mom and Jun took Pepper to the vet.
5. Pepper grew up.

Growing Up p. 47 Vocabulary

1. bought
2. scared
3. probably
4. people
5. pleasant
6. Shall
7. sign

Showing Good Manors p. 50

🎯 **COMPARE AND CONTRAST**

Possible responses: Good Manners: listening; Both: talking; Bad Manners: breaking promises.

Showing Good Manors p. 51 Vocabulary

1. b
2. f
3. e
4. a
5. g
6. d
7. c
8. Possible response: I promise I will not talk during class.

Dotty's Art p. 54

Possible responses given.

1. to teach how to make something
2. The author explains how Dotty made a dot picture.
3. to describe
4. The author tells about things in the picture.

Dotty's Art p. 55 Vocabulary

1. science
2. village
3. shoe
4. watch
5. guess
6. pretty
7. won

Living in Seoul p.58

DRAW CONCLUSIONS

1. c
2. d
3. a
4. b
5. Possible response: Children everywhere love to play games.

Living in Seoul p. 59 Vocabulary

faraway
parents
company
wash
answer
school
picture

Arachnid or Insect? p. 62

COMPARE AND CONTRAST

1. Possible response: Arachnids have eight legs and two body parts. Insects have antennae and wings.
2. Insects and arachnids are both small and can have hard shells.
3. Responses will vary but children should show similarities between two insects.
4. Responses will vary but children should show differences between two insects.

Arachnid or Insect? p. 63 Vocabulary

1. f
2. d
3. g
4. b
5. e
6. a
7. c
8. Possible response: When I was young, I would believe whatever anyone told me.

The International Food Fair! p. 66

SEQUENCE

1. c
2. a
3. e
4. d
5. b

The International Food Fair! p. 67 Vocabulary

1. d
2. e
3. g
4. f
5. a
6. c
7. b

Thomas Adams: Chewing Gum Inventor p. 70

FACT AND OPINION

1–3. Thomas Adams was born in 1818. Chicle is used in chewing gum and comes from Mexico. He had sons.
4–6. Adams was a well-dressed man. Chewing gum is better than wax gum. Adams best invention was chewing gum.

Thomas Adams: Chewing Gum Inventor p. 71 Vocabulary

1. f
2. e
3. a
4. g
5. b
6. d
7. c
8. Possible response: The only clothes I packed were too small!

Making Traveling Fun p. 74
DRAW CONCLUSIONS
Possible responses: Facts: Joe and Ann both made caves with blankets; Joe brought their favorite drinks; Ann was careful about the fruit she packed; Joe and Ann brought their favorite toys. Conclusions: Joe and Ann prepared for the car trip to make it more enjoyable and seem shorter.

Making Traveling Fun p. 74
clearing–Thing
crashed–Action Word
perfect–Describing Word
pond–Thing
splashing–Action Word
spilling–Action Word
traveled–Action Word

How Do Plants Grow? p. 78
SEQUENCE
1. d
2. b
3. c
4. a
5. e

How Do Plants Grow? p. 79 Vocabulary
1. e
3. c
3. b
4. d
5. a
Possible responses: bumpy: pickle, toad, bark; smooth: snake, apple, chalkboard

A Slice of Mud Pie p. 82
FACT AND OPINION
Possible responses:
Facts: Soil is made from sand grains, air, water, and humus; Sand grains are small particles of rock; Rain soaks into soil through small air spaces; Plants get water from the soil; Humus is made from plants and dead animals.
Opinions: Opinions will vary but should include a feeling or belief about soil.

A Slice of Mud Pie p. 83 Vocabulary
Make sure children find all the vocabulary words within the word search.

Too Many Frogs! p. 86
PLOT AND THEME
Possible response:
1. Josh wants a pet
2. Josh gets a frog, and decides he wants more frogs
3. Josh decides he has too many frogs, and only keeps one.
Sometimes too much of a good thing is a bad thing.

Too Many Frogs! p. 86 Vocabulary
1. f
2. g
3. d
4. e
5. a
6. b
7. c

Rainbow Crow Brings Fire to Earth p. 90
PLOT AND THEME
Possible responses: Problem: The snow and cold was making the animals suffer; Solution: Rainbow Crow brings back fire from the Great Spirit.
Responses will vary but should include: Rainbow Crow was given freedom because he gave up something important for his friends.

Rainbow Crow Brings Fire to Earth p. 90
Vocabulary
1. mountain
2. awaken
3. suffer
4. rainbow
5. prize
6. cliffs
7. volcano

Keeping Our Community Safe p. 94
FACT AND OPINION
1. Fact
2. Opinion
3. Opinion
4. Fact
5. Answers will vary but should include facts from *Keeping Our Community Safe.*

Keeping Our Community Safe p. 94
Vocabulary
buildings
quickly
roar
masks
burning
tightly
station

Annie Makes a Big Change p. 98
CAUSE AND EFFECT
1. Annie got mad.
2. Kids at school said Mrs. Potter was mean.
3. Mrs. Potter and Annie want to the land to be a park.
4. She got people to sign the petition.
5. The park was saved.

Annie Makes a Big Change p. 99 Vocabulary
Sentences will vary but should show understanding of vocabulary words.

Hubert and Frankie p. 102
PLOT AND THEME
Circled: 1, 2, 5.
1. middle
2. beginning
5. end

Hubert and Frankie p. 102 Vocabulary
1. wagged
2. grabbed
3. chewing
4. dripping
5. practice
6. treat
7. chased

Everyone Can Make a Difference! p. 106
CHARACTER AND SETTING
1. b
2. c
3. a
4. c
5. Responses will vary but should show that children understand and apply the story *Everyone Can Make a Difference!*

Everyone Can Make a Difference! p. 107
Vocabulary
1. clubhouse
2. greatest
3. wondered
4. climbed
5. truest
6. adventure
7. Exploring

Freda the Signmaker p. 110
MAIN IDEA
Responses will vary but should include that it is important to be organized and be supported with details from the paragraph.

Freda the Signmaker p. 111 Vocabulary
1. c
2. a
3. b
4. Possible response: I do not like to blame others when they make mistakes.
5. Possible response: Mary came up with an idea that helped us finish our important project.

Women Play Baseball p. 114
COMPARE AND CONTRAST
Possible responses:
Baseball: hit ball with bat, run around the bases
Both: women play
Soccer: kick ball, run up and down the field

Women Play Baseball p. 115 Vocabulary
cheers
Stories will vary but should include all vocabulary words.

American Revolution Heroes p. 118
AUTHOR'S PURPOSE
1. b
2. c
3. a
4. Responses will vary but should show an understanding of *American Revolution Heroes.*

American Revolution Heroes p. 119
Vocabulary
1. stripes
2. stars
3. freedom
4. America
5. nickname

A World of Birthdays p. 122
◎ DRAW CONCLUSIONS
Possible responses:
1. special foods, games, friends and family to celebrate
2. play different games; have different activities
3. Yes. They look happy in the pictures and they all say good things about their parties.

A World of Birthdays p. 123 Vocabulary
1. basket
2. favorite
3. bank
4. collects
5. aunt
6. presents
7. Possible response: My aunt collects stamps.

A Cowboy's Life p. 126
◎ SEQUENCE
Title: A Cowboy's Life
Characters: Carl Grigsby
Setting: The Lazy L Ranch in Texas. Events:
1. Carl got a job at the Lazy L Ranch herding cattle.
2. Carl rode on drive trails.
3. Barbed wire was invented and Carl worked on the fences.
4. Carl began riding in rodeos.

A Cowboy's Life p. 127 Vocabulary
1. herd
2. galloped
3. cowboy
4. trails
5. campfire
6. railroad

Voting Day p. 130
◎ FACTS AND DETAILS
1. underline
2. circle
3. underline
4. underline
5. circle
6–7. There are more parking lots than parks in their town. More people wanted a park more than a parking lot.

Voting Day p. 130 Vocabulary
1. mi/cro/phone
2. e/lec/tion
3. as/sem/bly
4. slogan
5. rallies
6. speeches